# Emotional Abuse in the Classroom

## —the forgotten dimension of safeguarding, child protection, and safer recruitment

## 2012 edition

## Requirements Analytics Publishing Programme 2012-2014

This list shows the topics of planned books. The final titles will be decided immediately prior to publication

- Analyzing Requirements, Systems, and Processes Summary
- Analyzing Requirements, Systems, and Processes Advanced
- Business Process Analysis
- Competence - analysis, dictionaries, management, and modelling
- Emotional Abuse in the Classroom
- Enterprise and Information Architectures
- ICE Regulations
- Information Systems
- Meta Meta Modelling
- Modelling with PSL-lite and PSL/PSA
- Normalization Introduction
- Normalization Advanced
- Object Property Relationship Modelling
- PSL-lite User Guide
- PSL/PSA User Guide
- Research Methods Essentials

Further information can be found on the Requirements Analytics website: requirementsanalytics.com

# Emotional Abuse in the Classroom

## the forgotten dimension of safeguarding, child protection, and safer recruitment

**Geoffrey Darnton**

**Requirements Analytics**

First edition 2012

Published by:
Requirements Analytics,
Suite 59
2 Lansdowne Crescent
Bournemouth, BH1 1SA
UK

http://ClassroomEmotionalAbuse.com/

ISBN: 978-1-909231-03-0 (paperback)
978-1-909231-04-7 (hardback)
978-1-909231-05-4 (eBook)

# Contents


## Preface v

Future Editions vii

## Chapter 1
## Introduction 1

Background 1
Book Structure 6

## Chapter 2
## What is Emotional Abuse? 11

Abuse 11
Emotion 11
Emotional+Abuse 12
Forms of Emotional Abuse 16
Abuser Motivations and Associations 19
Effects of Emotional Abuse 20
Abusers 21
Cultural causes 21

## Chapter 3
## Classroom Emotional Abuse 23

Scope 23
The Classroom 32

## Chapter 4
## Child Protection, Safeguarding and Safer Recruitment 39

Child Protection 39
Safeguarding 41
Safer Recruitment 46

**Chapter 5**
**Every Child Matters 49**

Critical Perspectives on ECM and Safeguarding 54
Children Rights Policy for Schools 64
Know What Your Schoolchildren Really Think 65

**Chapter 6**
**Teacher Self-Evaluation 69**

Psychological Abuse Scale For Teachers 69
Demeaning 70
Discriminating 71
Dominating 72
Destabilizing 73
Distancing 74
Diverse 75

**Chapter 7**
**Pupil Self-Evaluation 77**

Psychological Abuse Scale For Pupils 77
Questions Relating to Demeaning Conduct 78
Questions Relating to Discriminating Conduct 80
Questions Relating to Dominating Conduct 83
Questions Relating to Destabilizing Conduct 85
Questions Relating to Distancing Conduct 87
Diverse Questions 89

**Chapter 8**
**The Good, the Bad, and the Ugly... 91**

The Good ... 91
The Bad ... 92
The Ugly ... 92

**Appendix A**
**Definitions 93**

**Appendix B**
**International Declarations of the Rights of the Child 95**

Geneva Declaration of the Rights of the Child 95
UN Declaration of the Rights of the Child (UNDRC) 96
UNDRC Plain Language Version 99
UN Convention on the Rights of the Child (UNCRC) 100

**Appendix C**
**Draft School Child Rights Policy 129**

Purpose 130
Principles 130
Child Protection and Safeguarding 131
Education Rights 131
Freedom of Expression 132
Freedom of Thought, Conscience, and Religion 133
Rights of Assembly and Association 133
Rights of Privacy, Family Life, and Reputation 133
Right to Challenge Punishment and Detention 133
Right to Freedom from Exploitation 133
Special Educational Needs 134
Related Policies 134

**Appendix D**
**Wikipedia Articles 137**

**References 139**

**Index 145**

**Help with Training your People 152**

# Preface

Writing this book has been inspired by gaps I see in the child protection and safeguarding literature, practice, and procedures (specifically in the UK):

1. the current UK 'umbrella' framework, Every Child Matters, although it mentions emotional abuse, is very weak in addressing it;

2. there is a whole international world of debate about the rights of children, but for undisclosed policy reasons, has been left out of the mainstream Every Child Matters and safeguarding debates, even though the UK is under a legal obligation to implement the UN Convention on the Rights of the Child;

3. there is a lot of research indicating that perhaps even a majority of pupils have experienced some kind of emotional abuse in the classroom, by teachers (note: that is not a comment about a majority of teachers; it is a comment about the experiences of a majority of children). This is a phenomenon in many countries, not just the UK.

Therefore, the key purpose of this book is to discuss and explain those gaps, and provide professionals with some simple tools that may help in identifying and dealing with emotional abuse in the classroom. Having a strong academic vein in me, means that a secondary purpose is to provide pointers into relevant literature, so academics and students can take forward any of the issues raised.

Although the main context for this book is the UK, readers in other countries will benefit from the discussions of the various issues. Although terms such as 'Every Child Matters', and, 'safeguarding' are used extensively in the UK, other countries and cultures will have different terms for the same issues discussed.

My observations and thoughts have evolved over many years following a variety of roles in schools, including teaching, elements of school management, school governor, and formal responsibility as a governor for safeguarding in a school environment[1]. I have had many discussions with school pupils and ex-pupils over many years, and these have made me more conscious of the gaps mentioned above, because of the experiences of some of the pupils, and my realization

1 where Safeguarding was deemed 'outstanding' by OFSTED.

that they have had a very long-lasting impact, right through adulthood.

The life-long impact a teacher can have on a pupil, can be positive or negative—strong, and last for life. Many pupils and ex-pupils I have spoken with, have very positive memories associated with happy school days; others have recounted memories of unsupportive or abusive teacher conduct that has marked the ex-pupil for life.

I have also had the opportunity to discuss memories of school with a few ex-pupils who were caned[2]. The long-term impact of the caning is generally much less than the long term impact of some of the teacher emotional conduct towards pupils—generally that was much longer lasting, and had deeper impact. There really is a need to fill that gap of discussing teacher emotional behaviour in the classroom.

Humans can suffer abuse from many different sources. Much abuse is inflicted by others; some abuse is self-inflicted. In other situations, what may appear as abuse by others may be a personal response to the activities of others, in other words, a consequence of a person's own state of mind. Sorting these out is not easy at all, but when we act towards others, it is always important to keep in mind the possible or likely consequences.

Physical abuse is normally much easier to identify than emotional or psychological abuse. It is unwise to make general statements about the relative importance of different kinds of abuse, as each specific situation must be taken on its own merits. However, it is reasonable to say that emotional and psychological abuse can be much more long-lasting than physical abuse. This is a key theme of this book.

There is no doubt that debate about safeguarding, child protection, and safer recruitment makes it clear that emotional abuse is an issue to be dealt with. However, this book has been prepared out of an awareness that the safeguarding, child protection, and safer recruitment agendas have, in reality, been dominated primarily by concerns arising from a small number of serious cases of physical or sexual abuse (of course emotional abuse is involved in those also) or neglect, which have received considerable media and political attention. Physical abuse, sexual abuse, and neglect are so easy to portray and illustrate. Emotional abuse is much more difficult to portray and illustrate, yet its effects can be profound for an affected individual.

2 caned before corporal punished in schools in the UK was abolished, but ex-pupils in their 40s and 50s.

Also, there are not many diagnostic tools readily available for the professional, practitioner, or victim to use to check for the possible presence of emotional abuse or its effects.

This book is focussed on emotional abuse in the classroom. This is to provide a supplement to material that is more readily available and addressed to physical or sexual abuse, or neglect. The audiences are school teachers, responsible designated people who must ensure safeguarding and child protection, governors who must now receive some training in safeguarding, parents, and pupils.

This book is likely to be of greatest use to people who need to consider emotional abuse in the classroom in a practical sense. However, there is also an appropriate set of references with citations in the text so that those who wish to research the issues further, will find that the book also opens a window into different kinds of research that have a bearing on the subject matter, both legal and academic.

Geoffrey Darnton
*Bournemouth*
*September 2012*

**Future Editions**

Having observed, and experienced, that the impact of a good teacher can be life-long, and conversely, that the impact of a bad teacher can also be life-long, an original goal of this book was to present the results of some research into memorable school events.

That goal will not be met in this first edition of the book. I do have some field notes from discussions with pupils and ex-pupils, but not really enough to present yet. They would make a useful ethnographic contribution to the debate, but I am aiming for more.

Therefore, this edition of the book will be used to stimulate people to send in their stories and memories. Two chapters offer self-evaluation tools. Readers are encouraged to send in responses to those self-evaluation tools, or just to recount memories. Confidentiality of all material submitted, will be respected. There is a skeleton chapter which will be populated for the next edition of the book.

Thus, this edition of the book has avoided a chapter giving stories of teachers and children, or presenting empirical data on positive and negative school memories, or emotional abuse; it is dependent on other publications and research for concepts and ideas about prevalence.

Subsequent editions aim to go further. This edition of the book has as one aim (additional to filling the gaps identified above), the stimulation of responses from teachers and children about their classroom experiences. A future edition will summarize results - which will, hopefully, be updated for subsequent editions. Results will be both stories and statistics, suitable annonymized. Please write in with your own experiences and observations.

Although this book is specifically written to address emotional abuse in the classroom, it is essential that future editions also look at the obvious counterpart to that; what happens in classrooms to make children particularly happy, or to feel good. It will be enormously helpful for teachers to have information about things that have a positive effect on children; almost all teachers want their class children to have high learning attainment while being as happy as possible.

If you have written or published material which you feel should be used and referenced, please send in a copy of the relevant work. Where appropriate all relevant work submitted will be included in some way for future editions.

# Introduction

This book explores the issue of emotional abuse in the classroom. It proposes that although the issue is referred to in current official literature about child abuse, much more needs to be done, and it asserts that this kind of abuse, which may well be the most extensive and pervasive, does not receive the attention it needs. Emotional abuse is set within a context of all kinds of abuse, and within a context of official UK policy and steps to deal with abuse. Official context is considered in terms of sexual and physical abuse, Every Child Matters (ECM), child protection, and safer recruitment. Important gaps in ECM are set out, and a critical view of current official discourse about safeguarding etc., is taken. The concept of emotional abuse is explored and delimited. Its prevalence is identified. Self-diagnosing instruments are offered for teachers and pupils. It does not report any new research on relevant topics, but draws on a wide range of publications and research to inform the discussion. This book hopes to stimulate responses that can be used for further quantitative and qualitative research.

This book is focused quite specifically on one aspect of safeguarding and child protection, which receives little attention in discussions and training for those topics: emotional abuse in the classroom.

## Background

Debates and training about safeguarding and child protection in the UK have been focused primarily on sexual and physical abuse (and neglect), largely due to a very small number of high-profile cases that have been reported and investigated in the past few years. Unfortunate that those cases are, it is of great relief that such cases are very rare, notwithstanding the terrible backgrounds that emerge when they are investigated. It is noteworthy that these cases have happened notwithstanding the extensive and bureaucratic multi-agency contexts which have been built up over many years.

The 20th and 21st centuries have seen a dramatic reduction in certain kinds of abuse against children, particularly physical and sexual abuse. However, this book has been written with the aim of encouraging progress in dealing with the remaining problem of emotional abuse. More particularly, a whole range of professionals dealing with children and young people have professional responsibility to reduce as far as possible all kinds of abuse including emotional. As will be seen further in this document, the effects of emotional abuse in the classroom may well be far more pervasive and long-lasting to a significantly larger number of schoolchildren than the headline small number of cases over the past few years involving physical and sexual abuse, or neglect (and those cases are primarily outside the classroom or school context - but not entirely, hence Safer Recruitment policies).

Sexual and physical abuse are relatively easy to identify and deal with, although there are some boundary issues that still need more care and exploration, as discussed later.

The world has come a long way from the barbaric biblical suggestion that stubborn and rebellious children should be stoned to death (Deuteronomy 21: 18-21). Having ceased the practice of stoning wayward children to death, for many centuries other barbaric methods of punishing children continued right up to the present (and still continue in some places, legally or illegally).

Sexual abuse is reasonably well understood. In the UK the law has, ostensibly, been clarified by the Sexual Offences Act 2003 which in essence prohibits all sexual activity involving children below the age of 16. That act was in fact a rather odd piece of law in that it extended a prior prohibition of sexual intercourse by girls below the age of 16 to a prohibition of sexual activity below the age of 16. That was a significant extension of prohibition. Unsurprisingly, many adults, let alone children, fail to realize that since that 2003 Act, 'snogging' below the age of 16 is illegal, as well as sexual intercourse (Sawyer 2003). However, what is astonishing in terms of child protection and safeguarding is the almost total lack of enforcement of the law, other than in a very limited number of cases. This is one aspect safeguarding which virtually renders discussion of safeguarding to be schizophrenic. The incidence of teenage pregnancies below the age of 16 shows increasing breach of the legal prohibition of sexual intercourse below the age of 16. However, many professionals have managed to put themselves into a situation where teenage pregnancies are afforded considerable confidentiality notwithstanding the overt breach of the law. It is very difficult to comprehend how a girl below the age of 16 engaging activity that will result in pregnancy is not seen as evidence of a child seriously at risk, and therefore full safeguarding procedures should be applied. In addition, prosecution of those involved in creating pregnancies below the age of 16 is extremely rare. Therefore, the law prohibiting sexual activity below the age of 16 must, in a technical sense, be in disrepute. This is a very important sense in which safeguarding practices are completely out of line with prescriptions about safeguarding. This is, of course, a point Sawyer was attempting to address in her article (op. cit.). No wonder she suggests dropping the age of consent, but this would probably be unacceptable politically, so we must continue to muddle through with law that is followed much more in the breach than its enforcement.

Fortunately, this book does not need to address the question of sexual abuse any further (other than for comparative discussions) as it is concerned with emotional abuse, although it must be recognized that in many cases of underage pregnancy there is likely to be some considerable background that could be classed as emotional abuse, but most unlikely to be in the classroom. Teachers failing to act under safeguarding procedures in cases of underage pregnancies where the girl is aged between 13 and 16, are probably technical breaches of those safeguarding procedures. However, to be fair to the teachers, it is also likely that a teacher raising concerns about the sexual activities of a 13, 14, or 15 year-old, will often not receive support from other agencies.

At the crux of the debate about physical abuse remains the thorny issue of corporal punishment. In the UK, smacking (spanking) by parents is not, per se, illegal. It only becomes illegal when excessive or unreasonable force is used against a child. Corporal punishment in schools in the UK is now illegal, and in an increasing number of countries it is illegal in all contexts including by parents.

It is not very long ago since the corporal punishment of children could be extreme. There are many horrific accounts of institutionalized barbaric corporal punishment of children, young people, and adults. What is even more surprising, is that some of the recent literature that provides a foundation for discussing emotional abuse in schools gives examples of severe corporal punishment of children in schools (Hyman 1990). Indeed these cases were instrumental in creating greater pressure to change the law in the US, and resulted in more detailed focus on emotional abuse. In Europe, reformation of corporal punishment regimes and law started much earlier than in the US (earliest was 1783), prompted in part by the circulation of rather detailed and descriptive accounts of corporal punishment. It is ironic that the cane was introduced into English schools precisely because of emerging public sensitivities that it was not appropriate for male teachers to be smacking the naked bottoms of female pupils, but given the reality that any kind of clothing could reduce considerably the effects of smacking by hand, so the cane was selected as its effects could penetrate clothing. A cane can cause serious injury, as can the US paddle (US experiences are discuss in Hyman, 1997).

It is naïve to think that corporal punishment is always some act of hitting a child. Two of the most widely quoted writers on the subject have a broader definition:

"We believe that corporal punishment in the schools includes any disciplinary procedure intended to cause physical pain. This can include forcing ingestion of noxious foods as mentioned earlier, preventing children from going to the bathroom, forcing children to assume uncomfortable postures for extended periods or to spend long durations in a timeout chair or confined space, and imposing painful physical drills." (Hyman and Snook 1999, p31).

Therefore, although in institutional terms, problems with physical abuse in schools in many countries have been dealt with and clarified, in some countries problems remain. As implied by the previous quotation, there are some boundaries between physical and emotional abuse that are not clear, particularly when such a broader definition of corporal punishment is adopted.

One remaining problem with corporal punishment is that although it is sometimes characterized as physical abuse, there is a lot of evidence that in many instances it is difficult to separate completely from sexual abuse. This is because of the sexual gratification obtained by some participants in corporal punishment. Corporal punishment can involve a very complex set of effects, as yet under-researched although there is plenty of anecdotal evidence. An instance of corporal punishment involves the person inflicting the punishment, the person being punished, and may include witnesses to the event. Some instances of corporal punishment can have the effect of providing sexual gratification or arousal to any or all of perpetrator, victim or observer. Even if there is no sense of sexual gratification, the various participants may obtain some sense of enjoyment or pleasure from such events, even if it is only satisfying some prurient sense of curiosity by onlookers or providing opportunity for sadism.

Putting on one side sexual and physical abuse, the next area to consider is that of bullying, which may not involve either of these forms of abuse.

What is bullying? Another writer with experience of researching this topic suggests a definition of bullying:

"Bullying is when someone repeatedly and on purpose says or does mean or hurtful things to another person who has a hard time defending himself or herself.

The definition of bullying has three major components: first, it is aggressive behaviour that involves unwanted, negative actions. Second, bullying typically involves a pattern of behaviour repeated over time. Finally, it involves an imbalance of power or strength." (Olweus and Limber 2007) p11-12.

This definition of bullying is consistent with the concept of harassment as set out in the Protection from Harassment Act 1997, although a little narrower:

"1. Prohibition of harassment.

(1) A person must not pursue a course of conduct—

(a) which amounts to harassment of another, and

(b) which he knows or ought to know amounts to harassment of the other.

(2)For the purposes of this section, the person whose course of conduct is in question ought to know that it amounts to harassment of another if a reasonable person in possession of the same information would think the course of conduct amounted to harassment of the other."

Harassment in this legal definition only looks at the conduct; it does not require any imbalance of power or strength, therefore a teacher could harass a pupil, and equally, a pupil could harass a teacher, both of which are prohibited by law. A requirement for repetition only applies in the case of putting someone in fear of violence:

"4. Putting people in fear of violence.

(1) A person whose course of conduct causes another to fear, on at least two occasions, that violence will be used against him is guilty of

an offence if he knows or ought to know that his course of conduct will cause the other so to fear on each of those occasions."

Most school policies are focused on bullying of school pupils by school pupils. However, it should be clear that bullying can be applied more widely than this. Bullying could involve:

- pupils bullying pupils;
- pupils bullying teachers;
- teachers bullying pupils.

As will be seen below in the discussion about emotional abuse, it is almost certain that even if incidents of bullying do not involve sexual or physical abuse, they are likely to involve emotional abuse.

As this book is concerned with emotional abuse in the classroom it will not consider situations of pupils bullying pupils, or pupils bullying teachers. It will focus on teachers bullying pupils (but the possibility of the emotional abuse of teachers by pupils remains).

It is interesting that the author of the definition of bullying given earlier has the following advice to teachers:

"throughout this guide we have been careful to avoid using the terms "bully" and "victim" as much as possible when describing students who bully others or who are bullied by others. This is intentional, and we encourage you to avoid these labels as well, when talking with your students." (op. cit. p9).

In a similar vein, this book may use those terms, but leave it to the practitioner to contemplate the wisdom of using them.

## Book Structure

This first edition of the book is not large. It is hoped the next edition will be larger by incorporating experiences and results of feedback and questionnaires from teachers and pupils.

It is necessary to spend some effort in understanding several key terms in use with respect to things like punishment and abuse because there are problems in existing research and professional literature over the way those terms are used.

The title of the book itself contains the word 'abuse', which, as illustrated later, has specialized and general meanings.

However, the most important reason for issuing the book at this stage, is to start a debate about emotional abuse in the classroom, and provide simple instruments that can be used by teachers and pupils to explore their own experiences.

*Chapter 2* looks at the concept of emotional abuse. It starts from basics, examining definitions of emotion, abuse, and the two words put together. Early in the analysis, it is clear that he word abuse has two meanings; firstly, it has a general meaning, but secondly, it has rather specialized administrative and legal meanings as being unacceptable action that has crossed a threshold to justify some kind of state or official intervention. Different kinds of emotional abuse are identified. That is followed by looking at why some people abuse, and what is associated with such abuse. The effects of emotional abuse are noted. Finally, the chapter alerts readers to substantial cultural differences that relate to emotional abuse.

Following on from setting the scene of what is emotional abuse, *Chapter 3* moves on to the classroom. This chapter takes a careful look at terms such as punishment and abuse. Some literature distinguishes between physical and verbal punishment, or spanking and verbal punishment. After some discussion, punishment is defined and distinguished from retaliation and retribution. Some literature extends the concept of corporal punishment into a realm that does not involve any kind of hitting or striking or inflicting bodily pain which raises the spectre of forms of corporal punishment that sit with nonphysical punishment, retaliation, or retribution. Classroom shouting is explored briefly. Punishment is discussed in a context of moral development. The complex classroom environment is set out in terms of the key objectives arising from children being in the classroom. What kinds of behaviour are inappropriate in a classroom situation and what are the key problems of classroom discipline?

The increasing impact of modern technology and media on child expectations of classroom activity suggest a need to shift the classroom environment from traditional teaching, towards blended education and learning if pupils are not to become increasingly bored by a traditional classroom environment. A teacher self-evaluation questionnaire is introduced looking at the underpinning categories of potential classroom emotional abuse.

*Chapter 4* offers a brief look at what is the current UK context of child protection, safeguarding, and safer recruitment. These are specific terms used currently in the UK, so the terms themselves may be less meaningful to readers in other countries. Having said that, the issues are relevant in most countries, even if different terms are used elsewhere.

Child protection and safeguarding overlap, but are not the same things. To put it in somewhat simplistic terms, child protection is scoped as physical abuse, sexual abuse, neglect, and psychological abuse. Punishment is revisited briefly in a child protection context. As far as the classroom is concerned, the principal concern is the extent to which each child feels happy and safe. Any overlap between child protection and the classroom relates to the extent to which psychological and sexual abuse, and bullying, have slipped through the safeguarding and safer recruitment nets.

Statutory and government guidelines concerning safeguarding are discussed critically with respect to both government reorganizations and failures to address questions of emotional abuse in the classroom, and sexual abuse related to sexual activity of pupils. Safer recruitment procedures are discussed briefly.

To many professionals, the cornerstone of UK policy is based around a framework called Every Child Matters (ECM). *Chapter 5* takes a long hard look at ECM, and offers a supporting and critical review. Although many writers and professionals pin the development of ECM to one critical child protection case (Victoria Climbié), it is clear that that case and its subsequent inquiry report were a catalyst for many issues that had been building up before the case - to which were added specific issues arising from that particular case. Thus, ECM has a far wider agenda than the official inquiry report for the case. The chapter discusses how ECM (and the related Children Act 2004) have failed to deal with more general socioeconomic issues, putting most focus on individual children and their families.

The UK has ratified the UN Convention on the Rights of the Child (UNCRC). However, nothing about child rights has found its way into ECM. There is now a Children's Commissioner who is guided by the UNCRC. The chapter discusses the uncomfortable coexistence of ECM and UNCRC. The proposal is that schools adopt a Children Rights Policy to supplement the policies adopted by virtue of ECM (and hence child protection, safeguarding, and safer recruitment).

Having presented some difficult and complex material in the first chapters of the book, *Chapter 6* moves on by offering a very practical self-evaluation tool that can be used by teachers to assess whether or not they engage in any classroom conduct that could result in abuse.

This tool is included by kind permission of its developer, Prof. W.C. Nesbit who has researched the issue of classroom emotional abuse by teachers.

The impatient teacher reader could simply start with this chapter It is a simple presentation of Nesbit's questions according to his 6 Ds. A teacher can simply read those questions and answer them mentally, reflecting on their significance, and perhaps noting any classroom style adjustments that suggest themselves.

An original goal of the book was to present child experiences of the classroom. A lot of ethnographic material has been collected, but not yet enough. Therefore more will be collected for the next edition of the book. *Chapter 7* has taken the teacher self-evaluation questionnaire from Chapter 6 and 'inverted' it for use by pupils or ex-pupils. Many of the questions have been created simply by asking respondents if they have experienced certain things in the classroom, as indicated in the questionnaire. Further questions have been added to enhance the inverted questions.

Chapter 8, the final chapter, is really a 'stub' chapter. It shows the categories of material to be included in the next edition of the book. The material will be classified as the good, the bad, and the ugly. The chapter discusses what these are, giving simple examples of the kinds of situations that would be in each class. Readers are encouraged to write in with their stories, and also encourage other to write in. Talk about both good experiences that really made you feel good, and the bad.

Following on from the chapters, are some appendices.

*Appendix A* brings together some key definitions that have been developed in various chapters of the book. Some readers may not agree with the specific definitions given, but that doesn't matter. Alternative terms can be used. Having those definitions will help the reader to unpack some of the words used by various writers.

One important theme in the book is the way ECM has left out any child rights arising from the UK ratifying the UNCRC. Because the omission is so glaring, it must be assumed that there have been policy decisions to procrastinate over bringing child rights into UK domestic law. This assumption is even more likely given that one recommendation about that, from the Victoria Climbié inquiry report was simply ignored in the formal government response. Given the serious gap in ECM over child rights, *Appendix B* sets out the wording of three key international documents about child rights. They will help schools that wish to develop a child rights policy.

*Appendix C* offers a template Children Rights Policy that schools can consider adopting. Doubtless, different schools will wish to adopt varying emphases. Hence Appendix C can be used as an important resource while schools consider what to include in their Children Rights Policy.

There is a lot of doubt in the academic world about Wikipedia. The number of times I have seen academics write comments on student work about how the student shouldn't use Wikipedia as a reference! That is discussed further in *Appendix D*. Also, Appendix D contains pointers to articles in Wikipedia. Many of those Wikipedia articles open windows into important and relevant literature, so those who need a more academic approach to the topics discussed in the book can identify readily many more sources.

Happy reading, as the book now moves on to discuss emotional abuse.

# What is Emotional Abuse?

'Emotional abuse' is one of those terms everyone understands—until trying to define it!

Let's start by unpacking the term into its two constituent parts: 'abuse', and, 'emotional'.

## Abuse

The Oxford English Dictionary (OED, 2009), in its usual and thorough style, give a variety of meanings for the word, not all of which we need to worry about for an operational understanding of 'abuse' as inferred by 'emotional abuse'.

Abuse can be a noun or a verb. When used in the term 'emotional abuse' it is clearly being used as a noun. There is a slight irony in that the OED definitions as a verb are slightly more helpful to the purposes of this book than as a noun. Use as a modern word such as related to sexual or other maltreatment is shown as a 1993 addition to the dictionary, suggesting that qualification by an adjective such as 'emotional' is a relatively recent development.

Two of the OED entries for use as a verb are directly to the point: " To ill-use or maltreat; to injure, wrong, or hurt"; " To wrong with words; to speak injuriously of or to; to malign, revile".

Webster's Dictionary (Gove, 2002) is much briefer than the OED in its discussion of abuse, but with a first entry directly to the point: " to attack or injure with words : reproach coarsely : DISPARAGE <abuse a person in the most violent terms> b obsolete : to speak falsely of : MISREPRESENT <abused her to her friends>".

## Emotion

The most appropriate understanding of the term 'emotion' in the OED (2009) is: "Psychology. A mental 'feeling' or 'affection' (e.g. of pleasure or pain, desire or aversion, surprise, hope or fear, etc.), as distinguished from cognitive or volitional states of consciousness. Also abstr. 'feeling' as distinguished from the other classes of mental phenomena".

For Webster's Dictionary: " the affective aspect of consciousness: FEELING <we are not men of reason, we are creatures of emotion— C.C.Furnas> b : a reaction of or effect upon this aspect of consciousness <the essential emotion of the play is the feeling of a son toward a guilty mother— T.S.Eliot> <the emotion of beauty, like all our emotions, is certainly the inherited product of unimaginably countless experiences in an immeasurable past— P.E.More> <reason rather than emotion forms the main basis for his marriage— Nellie Maher> <the mind must have its share in deciding these important matters, not merely the emotions and desires— Rose Macaulay>" (Gove, 2002).

## Emotional+Abuse

This initial, somewhat pedantic, look at the words is done because there is as yet no clear professional meaning to the term 'emotional abuse' in the literature. Indeed, as will be seen shortly, use of the term can be very restricted due to welfare and legal consequences of using the word 'abuse'. Therefore, it is helpful to start the discussion with an operational definition.

It is also important to keep in mind that for many writers, terms such as 'emotional abuse', 'psychological abuse', 'emotional aggression', 'psychological aggression' are, to all intents and purposes, synonymous. There is far clearer separation in the literature between physical and emotional (or psychological) abuse.

There are some useful definitions in the literature (this is not a systematic survey, but just some examples):

- "Emotional Abuse: Undermining an individual's sense of self-worth and/or self-esteem is abusive. This may include, but is not limited to constant criticism, diminishing one's abilities, name-calling, or damaging one's relationship with his or her children." (USDOJ, 2012)
- "Emotional abuse is the systematic diminishment of another. It may be intentional or subconscious (or both), but it is always a course of conduct, not a single event. It is designed to reduce a child's self-concept to the point where the victim considers himself unworthy—unworthy of respect, unworthy of friendship, unworthy of the natural birthright of all children:

love and protection. (Vachss, 1994)

- In discussing definitions of emotional abuse, "psychological abuse is the denial of essential psychological nutrients or the denigration of personal worth through domination techniques and patterns of interaction which are damaging to the emerging personality" (Nesbit, 1991)
- Emotional abuse is the persistent emotional maltreatment of a child such as to cause severe and persistent adverse effects on the child's emotional development. It may involve conveying to children that they are worthless or unloved, inadequate, or valued only insofar as they meet the needs of another person. It may include not giving the child opportunities to express their views, deliberately silencing them or 'making fun' of what they say or how they communicate. It may feature age or developmentally inappropriate expectations being imposed on children. These may include interactions that are beyond the child's developmental capability, as well as overprotection and limitation of exploration and learning, or preventing the child participating in normal social interaction. It may involve seeing or hearing the ill-treatment of another. It may involve serious bullying (including cyberbullying), causing children frequently to feel frightened or in danger, or the exploitation or corruption of children. Some level of emotional abuse is involved in all types of maltreatment of a child, though it may occur alone (DCSF, 2010).

A key difficulty in establishing a definition of emotional abuse concerns the threshold at which various jurisdictions will consider that state intervention is appropriate. As can be imagined, the threshold for state intervention is higher than the recognition of the phenomenon itself, because of the usual state requirement for a minimum level of severity before intervention is considered necessary or appropriate.

This problem is discussed carefully by Straus and Field (2003): "We have avoided using the term psychological *abuse* for the parental behaviour described in this article. One reason is that abuse is used in overlapping but different ways. It can refer to a judgment based on informal social norms and also to a legal or administrative category for purposes of welfare services or criminal intervention...In principle, to be legally or administratively classified as abusive requires that the behavior exceed a level of severity and chronicity that a caseworker or criminal justice official believes puts the child at risk". Although their discussion is concerned with parental behaviour, the same considerations are at play with respect to teacher behaviour.

For example, some definitions used as a basis for possible state intervention are:

- "Emotional abuse is the persistent emotional ill-treatment of a child such as to cause severe and persistent adverse effects on the child's emotional development. It may involve conveying to children that they are worthless or unloved, inadequate, or valued only insofar as they meet the needs of another person." This is used in the UK (Wilson and James, 2007).
- Pennsylvania defines psychological maltreatment as "serious mental injury" (Hyman and Snook, 1999).

The difficulties of defining emotional abuse are discussed by McEachern, Aluede, and Kenny (2008) who provide a helpful set of pointers to other literature that has also attempted to do so.

Straus and Field (2003) offer a helpful baseline against which policy and decisions could be based: "An alternative hypothesis is based on the theory that any act of psychological aggression against a child, regardless of whether the aggression is a purely expressive emotional outburst or is a means of correcting and controlling misbehaviour puts the child at increased risk for mental disabilities... If this hypothesis is supported, it means that any psychological aggression is abusive".

As the number of acts of psychological aggression increases, the risk of social and psychological problems is also likely to increase.

From such a 'base zero', it should be possible to establish thresholds for interventions such as professional intervention in a teacher setting, or welfare or criminal intervention in any setting.

There is a lot of research evidence that psychological aggression is harmful to children.

In determining policy, should there be zero tolerance? Do social norms permit some psychological aggression? At what thresholds should various forms of intervention be contemplated? To adapt a sentence from Straus and Field, "Teachers can and should criticize misbehaviour, but they should do so by criticizing the behaviour, and not the child as a person".

Part of the problem in deciding thresholds is that psychological 'pain' is an inherent part of life (people cannot always have what they want, and they cannot always do what they wish). Pain arising from frustration at not getting or doing something wanted is probably not damaging, whereas pain arising from an emotional attack on the child may be.

Emotion is feelings, contrasted with reason in several of the quoted uses, so that is a helpful starting point.

Emotional abuse can be taken to be maltreat, injure or hurt using words (that gives clear contrast with physical abuse).

Therefore an initial operational definition can be contemplated: Emotional abuse is to maltreat, injure, or hurt someone's feelings, by words or expressions, .

Of course, there is a subjective element in abuse defined this way, because people vary in their response to the words and expressions of another. Indeed, taken to its extreme, there are people who believe that it is never the case that someone else can injure our feelings; injury arises because of our own reactions to someone else's words or expressions. In that sense we injure ourselves; we can develop resistance to the words and expressions of others. This suggests a need to qualify the definition by introducing a term such as 'reckless' (a term in common use in the legal world, and hence a term that is easier in the event that some judicial or quasi-judicial interpretation is needed).

In other words, because we cannot know another person's emotional reactions to our emotional words or expressions until we know that person better, but still proceed with potentially maltreating, injurious, or hurtful words or expressions we are being reckless if there is a possibility of maltreatment, injury, or hurt to someone's feelings. Also, what may, *prima facie*, be potentially harmful words or expressions, may be used with friends in jest, in humour, or with a genuine sense of endearment and familiarity—but we need to know the person and their likely reactions first!

As discussed further below, reactions by one person to the words and expressions of another are likely to be highly dependent on the context of the relationship between those two people; are they peers? - are they in an intimate relationship? - is there a high power distance? - are they separating from a previous close relationship?

Therefore, the operational definition of emotional abuse evolves to something like: **"emotionally abusive behaviour is the use of words or expressions directed at other people, reckless (or intentional) as to the possibility of maltreatment, injury or hurt to those others".**

Whether actual maltreatment, injury or hurt takes place requires a subjective test because different people react differently. The recklessness or intention is much more an objective test because the abuser has not considered, or actually intends, the possibility of maltreatment, injury or hurt to someone else.

In the same way that a person who delivers corporal punishment to another, may obtain some personal gratification from inflicting the punishment, or genuinely believes the punishment is a duty, the same difficulty can arise with verbal or expressive admonishment; the person doing the act obtains some personal gratification from doing so, or genuinely believes the admonishment is a duty.

Physical abuse is nearly always preceded and accompanied by emotional abuse of some kind, but emotional abuse is not always followed by physical abuse. There are many situations where an abuser using emotional abuse will not go as far as physical abuse, for a variety of reasons, and restraint mechanisms. However, there is often an increased risk that an emotional abuser wants to go on to physical abuse, and would do so in the absence of restraints.

## Forms of Emotional Abuse

Many forms of emotional abuse are enumerated in the literature. If brought together, there would be many synonyms and homonyms, and a great deal of overlap between the concepts. Therefore, for the purposes of this book, it is unnecessary to attempt an academic survey and synthesis of those, with a formal critical review of the literature; it is sufficient to set out many forms of emotional abuse, as most people will have no difficulty recognizing them, even though they may have difficulty if challenged to provide a formal definition.

Generally, the literature identifies these as forms of emotional abuse because of their *potentia*l to cause harm in a recipient child, independently of one's view about harm being caused by others, or by self-reaction to the words and expressions of others. Whether or not actual harm results will always be a matter of establishing facts.

In considering all of these, always keep in mind the likely effect of context between a person using the words or expressions, and the recipient of them. This book is primarily concerned with classroom situations. Therefore the most likely context is a teacher and children in the teacher's care. Having said that, much of the useful literature is focussed on parent and child; there is much less literature and research about teacher and child.

One of the most common and pervasive forms is shouting. Indeed, as far as parenting is concerned, there are some clear social norms as far as the US is concerned, as pointed out by Straus and Field (2003): "Prevalence rates greater than 90% and the absence of differences according to child or family characteristics suggests that psychological aggression is a near universal disciplinary tactic of American parents". They also report high levels of psychological aggression between intimate partners.

There is insufficient research about teacher shouting in classes to understand why some teachers do that. Shouting must be considered to be a form of aggression, and in the family research literature is certainly considered to be a form of punishment (verbal punishment), sometimes contrasted with physical punishment such as spanking (for example, see Berlin et al., 2009).

When a teacher shouts in a classroom, there are several possible explanations:

- it is a normal form of emotional expression for that particular teacher;
- the teacher is experiencing limitations to their own anger management;
- the teacher believes that shouting is an effective way to secure child compliance with directions

Of course, many children can be concerned when a teacher shouts. A child reaction can be to dislike the teacher or lead to teacher avoidance behaviour. Some teacher shouting can engender fear of the teacher. It can also result in diminished respect for the teacher by the pupils, sometimes even to the point of ridicule.

A teacher may give arbitrary, unpredictable, or inconsistent instructions. When accompanied by instructions to comply, this can cause real concern to children.

There are different ways in which a child can be ignored by a teacher:

- a particularly quiet child may be left to be quiet; a teacher should try to apply as much inclusiveness as possible, and ensure that a quiet child is not being hurt by being left out of various activities;
- a child may want to participate in discussion or responses to a teacher's questions, but the teacher regularly ignores the child;
- a child may be isolated;
- a child may ask a teacher for particular advice or information, but the teacher declines to provide it;
- the teacher, for some reason, wishes to reject or ostracize a child.

Sarcasm can be a particular teacher style that does not go down well with pupils.

Most of the examples given so far, fall more into a grey area in terms of whether they constitute abuse or not. Certainly, objective tests of abuse would produce highly variable results. However, keep in mind that what really matters, is not objective tests, but subjective tests in terms of the actual effects on actual children. Failing to consider those, is a form of recklessness, and as such, falls into the abuse camp.

There are other forms of teacher behaviour that are much less in a grey area, and for more likely to constitute emotional abuse.

A pupil may be singled out for specific attention by a teacher, sometimes in front of other class pupils, and be subjected to ridicule, humiliation, and denigration.

Sometimes a child can be on the receiving end of name-calling, putdowns, insults, threats, and even bullying.

A teacher may express bigotry about specific beliefs that could be in contradiction to some beliefs of some of the children.

One form of abusive behaviour that is more difficult to perpetrate in a whole-class environment, but can be effective with individual children, is 'gaslighting'. This can take a variety of forms such as providing false information, denying that certain events happened (when they did), asserting that certain events happened (when they didn't), or engaging in disorientating behaviour leading a child or children to doubt their own recollection or memory.

A teacher may gossip about a child to others (teachers, parents, or pupils).

Thus, abuse can take many different forms. All the examples given in this section have been drawn from research literature exploring forms of emotional or psychological aggression. Many are applicable to both home and school settings.

There is a serious lack of research into the prevalence of all possible forms of classroom abuse. However, there does seem to be a general consensus that emotional abuse in the classroom is far more prevalent and extensive than physical or sexual abuse which have driven much of the school child protection policy debates and legislation. In part, this is because of much greater confusion in social norms about emotional and psychological abuse.

## Abuser Motivations and Associations

Why do abusers abuse? As mentioned above, on an initial classification, abusers are demonstrating some aspect of their personality, or they may genuinely believe, even though erroneously, that their conduct really is in the interests of the child.

Some abusers have characteristics that can cause serious harm to children. The abusers may or may not be aware of this, and may be in denial if aware of the possibility.

In terms of emotional abuse in the classroom, there is insufficient substantive research for certainty, therefore it is necessary to speculate, while being informed by other research in similar contexts.

There is a power imbalance in the classroom. In the same way that some child sexual abusers seek out opportunities for contact with children, there will be some emotional abusers who seek out power imbalance situations that give them control, or a sense of control, over children.

It is the existence of a power imbalance that can be an important element in an abusive relationship. The same is true for power imbalance in family situations.

One obvious element in such a power imbalance situation is that the abuser feels sufficient freedom to express verbal aggression. Children may feel unable to stop it, and peers may be very reluctant to try to deal with it.

Enjoying a power imbalance situation and expressing verbal aggression are forms of dominating behaviour. Many abusers obtain some satisfaction from expressing dominating behaviour.

Emotional abuse can also be associated with attempting to control by fear, jealousy, manipulative behaviour, and projection (where the abuser projects their personality characteristics onto the victim).

## Effects of Emotional Abuse

It is difficult to separate emotional abuse from mental or psychological abuse as many writers use these terms interchangeably, but in any event there is some relevant research, but much more is needed. Also, please keep in mind that it is beyond the scope of this book to present a detailed summary of the relevant research; that may be added in a later edition if there is sufficient demand. Some examples of research are identified.

The reported possible effects of emotional abuse include psychological trauma, anxiety, depression, post-traumatic stress disorder, self-doubt, loss of self-confidence, anger, alexithymia (difficulty identifying and processing own emotions), victim blaming (self-blaming).

One leading researcher in the field (Hyman, 1990) has researched what he terms 'Educator-Induced Post Traumatic Stress Disorder' (EIPTSD). One of his points is that "children are more vulnerable to less extreme stressors than those that may cause PTSD [Post Traumatic Stress Disorder] in adults. Other researchers have taken EIPTSD and researched it further. In an interesting study of teachers who had received physical or psychological abuse when they were children, 40-60% of the teachers had experienced stress symptoms because of being abused by their own teachers. Another study to understand EIPTSD further found that forms of abuse included ridicule, overly punitive sanctions, verbal assaults, physical assault, isolation or rejection, verbal discrimination, peer humiliation, and corruption.

There are many sources of information about the effects of abuse. One useful summary of the psychological consequences of maltreatment is Erickson and Egeland (1987), although they cover maltreatment wider than emotional. They summarize the effects according to several researchers in the field, including Kempe's work that started the 'battered child syndrome' awareness that drove so much public policy at that time. Another useful source is McEachern, Aluede and Kenny (2008).

## Abusers

There is conflicting evidence about the prevalence of emotional abusers among males and females. Several studies report a higher incidence of psychological aggression or abuse among females than males, but other studies conclude that males are more likely to be abusers than females.

The bottom line, is that sex is not a good predictor of a tendency to be an emotional abuser. It seems that a range of personality traits are better predictors, such as high rates of suspicion and jealousy; sudden and drastic mood swings; poor self-control, higher than average rates of approval of violence, and higher levels of some personality disorders.

Of course, although this book is primarily concerned with emotional abuse in the classroom, with emphasis on emotional abuse by teachers against children, it should not be forgotten that emotional abusers can include some school-children themselves, who may be abusers of their peers, or teachers.

There is little research about the characteristics of classroom abusers. This is not surprising, as it would require identifying abusers in order to study them!

Later in the book, there is a self-evaluation instrument built from research about classroom abuse, which teachers can use to evaluate the extent to which they display any behaviours that could be considered to be abusive.

## Cultural causes

Social, cultural and religious norms may be critical in understanding the effect of one person's words or expressions on another person.

Many variables (racial, ethnic, cultural and subcultural, nationality, religion, family dynamics, mental illness, etc.) make it difficult or impossible to define roles in any meaningful way that apply to the entire population. Behaviour that may cause harm to children in one culture, may not have the same effect in another culture.

A major difficulty in writing this book and accessing relevant literature, is that it is the infrastructures of the developed world that have supported much of the published research. There is a real scarcity of cross-cultural research making generalizations based on existing research, particularly hazardous.

There are some pieces of research that have attempted cross-cultural studies of direct relevance to the subject matter of this book, and although far from definitive, the one key message is that there are substantial cross-cultural differences in the use of physical and emotional punishments and the reactions of children to those punishments.

Two examples of such cross-cultural research are the work of Berlin et al. (2009) who include white, African American and Mexican American people in the research, and, Benbenishty and Astor (2005) who report differences between Israeli and Arab people. Both of these examples include cultural differences that are statistically significant. In contrast, the work of Straus and Field (2003), as noted earlier, report psychological aggression as a near universal disciplinary tactic by American parents.

Therefore, it is imperative that readers of this book sensitize themselves to the likelihood of substantial differences between cultures. In doing so, it is important to keep in mind the dangers of using nationality as a proxy for culture.

Hofstede, Hofstede, and Minkov (2010) present a summary of several studies comparing cultures on a range of dimensions. Relevant to the points made above, there are deep cultural differences, which will undoubtedly impact whether or not a particular classroom situation can be considered abusive or not. For example, there are important differences on the individualistic-collectivistic dimension concerning the appropriateness of conveying emotions by facial expressions.

No attempt is made to define the term 'culture' as used in this book, but it can certainly be observed that it would be very unwise to use nationality as a proxy for culture because of the huge cultural diversity in many countries. For a much deeper understanding of 'culture', use a book such as Hofstede, Hofstede, and Minkov, avoiding material where nationality is used as a proxy for culture.

# Classroom Emotional Abuse

The previous chapter set out the concept of emotional abuse, along with summary information about its effects, some characteristics of abusers, and the importance of cultural context. This chapter focuses the discussion on emotional abuse in the classroom.

## Scope

There are several words likely to be used in relation to confrontational situations. These include abuse, punishment, defence, retaliation, restraint, disagreement, and debate. A recurrent theme in the relevant research literature is the restricted reliability and validity of some studies because of a failure to define terms sufficiently. For example, Berlin et al. (2009) note "...as several scholars have noted [list of several scholars], many studies have investigated spanking without defining the term, nor asked for parents' own definitions".

The word 'abuse' is somewhat loaded to many people because it normally carries a connotation of wrong action that can cause harm. That is why some writers prefer to talk about punishment rather than abuse. For example, Berlin et al. (2009) refer to 'spanking and verbal punishment'. There are many genuine and appropriate debates to be had whether some action is punishment or abuse (or both), because of the presence in some people, of ideological decisions such as physical punishment is always abusive.

Similar issues arise concerning matters as simple as debate and discussion. If a teacher and pupil are having a discussion and they disagree about an issue, is there a point where teacher insistence on being correct and denying the pupil further discussion, particularly when it is the teacher who is wrong about the issue, becomes an abuse of the power imbalance situation? There are big differences between statements such as "we don't have enough time to continue this discussion, because there are other things that need to be done", "we will have to agree to differ on this", and, "just be quiet - I'm the teacher and know better".

There are temporal matters related to these identified terms.

Defence is at the time of an event; retaliation is after an event. Restraint is also at the time of an event. Punishment is after an event. Disagreement and debate are events. Abuse is an event.

The most difficult differentiation to make, is that between punishment and abuse. Punishment as a term has been looked at and discussed carefully by Hyman and Snook (1999). They offer a very simple definition of **punishment** as "**...a procedure that decreases the chance that a misbehaviour will recur**". This is a very important definition in that it separates punishment from retribution. In that sense, it is a more modern interpretation of the word because dictionary definitions have a clear link between punishment and retribution - to the point they could be considered synonymous.

However, in an educational setting, it is very important to distinguish between a procedure that is retributive and a procedure that is designed to deter a repetition of undesired behaviour. There is the added nuance that retribution also has a sense of paying back, or making good.

There is an important difference between "I will spank you because you hit Johnny", and, "because you hit Johnny, I will spank you so you know what will happen if you hit him again, and to encourage you not to hit him again". This goes to the heart of many attitudes towards punishment. Some people have an attitude "because you did that, you must be punished"; is this really "because you did that, you must receive retribution"? If Mary hits Johnny and is spanked for that, following which she never hits him again, it *may* be that she does not hit him again because of punishment avoidance; there may be other reasons, such as she has internalized a belief that she should not hit. However, if she hits him again after being spanked, the spanking may not have been a procedure that decreased the chance the hitting will recur - it would be necessary to examine the dynamics between Mary and Johnny to know whether the chance of hitting him had decreased, but Johnny had actually been much more provocative to Mary. However, all other things being equal, if Mary hits Johnny again after being spanked for it, the spanking clearly did not have the desired effect. Therefore further spanking of Mary becomes retribution at least, and risks becoming abusive. Hyman and Snook make a similar point with respect to what they call 'deprivation punishment', of which they cite 'time out' (removing the child from a positive situation, typically placed in isolation). What is important about this, is that they include such deprivation punishment as a form of corporal punishment, but which is not also direct retribution.

Hyman and Snook offer a definition of corporal punishment: "... any disciplinary procedure intended to cause physical pain". Having studied many examples of corporal punishment, they give a list of procedures they considered included: "forcing ingestion of noxious foods, preventing children from going to the bathroom, forcing children to assume uncomfortable postures for extended periods or to spend long durations in a time-out chair or confined space, and imposing painful physical drills".

The inclusion by Hyman and Snook of deprivation punishment as a special case of corporal punishment, does suggest problems of definition.

Going back to basics, the term 'corporal' relates to the human body (OED, 2009; Gove, 2002). Clearly, procedures such as deprivation punishment are not inflicting pain in the normal bodily sense. Therefore, there is a need for three concepts of punishment, rather than two:

1. corporal punishment - with physical pain
2. corporal punishment - without physical pain
3. non-corporal punishment

This means redefining corporal punishment as "any disciplinary procedure involving the body". That would include Hyman and Snook's 'deprivation punishment' and procedures such as time-out, exclusion, and isolation. Of course, some people will not agree with including deprivation punishment as a form of corporal punishment. For the purpose of this book it is included. The book is successful if it help readers to sort out a set of operational definitions for the reader's purposes.

There are situations where some procedure is used, but clearly the procedure is not a punishment as defined above, if there is no realistic likelihood that the procedure will reduce the chance that a misbehaviour or undesired behaviour will recur. For such situations, it is probably better to use a term such as 'preventative disciplinary procedure'. Hence, many instances of exclusion or isolation are really preventative disciplinary procedures rather than corporal punishment without physical pain; such a procedure may start life motivated as a punishment, but clearly if problems persist, the procedure becomes either a preventative disciplinary procedure, retribution, or abuse.

Having unpacked corporal punishment, it is interesting to explore the phenomenon of a teacher shouting in a classroom.

Is this a procedure that is simply representative of a common expressive style of the teacher? Is the shouting directed at the whole class, or individual pupils? Is it an attempt to secure the attention of the class over a noisy classroom?

Some literature refers to verbal punishment. For example, Berlin et al. (2009) define verbal punishment as "....scolding, yelling, or derogating,...".

Obviously, many children do not like adults scolding or shouting at them, and will respond as though it is a punishment (i.e. they will change behaviour to avoid a repeat punishment). However, a teacher needs to be on more certain ground: "if you do that, I will punish you by shouting at you....". This needs some understanding of the child involved. Some children will respond appropriately; some will not. Indeed, some children may see that as a teacher weakness and provoke the teacher further (in some cultures, expressing anger and shouting are seen as real weaknesses, and respect for the person shouting or expressing anger, is lost).

The main point here is that, in terms of the definitions above, non-corporal punishment may well be perceived as something other than punishment. What is not understood so well, is any mechanisms involved.

Without getting into a long academic or philosophical debate in this book, theories of moral development may provide some help in unpacking non-corporal punishment procedures. For example, Kohlberg's (1981) six stages of moral development provide a framework within which all the kinds of punishment described above, may fit. They suggest that although non-corporal punishment procedures such as shouting in class by a teacher may be less effective in terms of punishment avoidance, they may contribute to higher levels of moral development. Having said that, there is a high chance that teacher shouting is more to do with the teacher's mode of expression rather than being a rationally devised punishment procedure. Effectiveness in terms of moral development theories would also require that the teacher has a good understanding of the current stage of moral development of the children. In the absence of such knowledge of the children who are being shouted at, there is a very high risk that teacher shouting is then reckless, and thus falls into the category of abusive behaviour.

This book will be read by people in a variety of legal jurisdictions concerning the punishment of children in both home and school.

In terms of the definitions above, the main issue for different legal jurisdictions concerns the matter of corporal punishment with physical pain. As we saw, the term corporal punishment is a bit too wide.

For jurisdictions that prohibit forms of corporal punishment, the other main difference is whether the prohibition applies only to schools, or if it extends to other places such as the home. Corporal punishment without physical pain is much less likely to be outlawed. Similarly, preventative disciplinary procedures may not be outlawed, but in some jurisdictions, may be regulated (for example, the regulation in the UK of school exclusions). Different jurisdictions address the matter of school attendance in different ways also. In many jurisdictions, school attendance is compulsory. In some jurisdictions it is full-time education that is compulsory rather than school attendance (for example, the UK).

Thus, we have a complex set of words that different people will interpret differently: punishment; retribution; retaliation.

This means that policy formulation in an educational setting needs to be careful about what procedures it has, and what they are called.

Leaving punishment defined as earlier (a procedure intended to reduce the likelihood of repeat misbehaviour), a word is needed for a procedure that simply inflicts something normally undesirable in return for having misbehaved, independently of any assessment that the procedure will reduce the likelihood of a repeat offence. An appropriate word for that is retaliation. If there is a procedure whereby an offender is supposed to make up for the effects of the offence, an appropriate word would be retribution.

Mary hits Johnny. Punishment: Mary is spanked in the hope that by doing so, she will not hit Johnny again. Retaliation: Mary is spanked. Retribution: Mary must do something that helps or supports Johnny.

This can be repeated for a situation where only verbal punishment is used, rather than spanking: Mary hits Johnny. Punishment: Mary is shouted at in the hope that by doing so, she will not hit Johnny again. Retaliation: Mary is shouted at. Retribution: Mary must do something that helps or supports Johnny.

The need for a more careful definition and use of terms is not only helpful for policy formulation; it is helpful for research because of the many comments in relevant research papers that much research suffers from loosely defined terms. There is much that is not known about the outcomes from different procedures to deal with what is defined as misbehaviour. Of course, different people will prefer to use those words differently. The point is to have policies that are clear and well defined.

A much deeper problem that can have a major impact on whether procedures are abusive, is the definition of what constitutes misbehaviour.

A classroom is a highly complex environment in which at least three things are taking place: (1) inculcation of certain behaviours, norms, and beliefs; (2) facilitating child learning in one way or another and for a variety of reasons; (3) providing a child-minding service.

It is in respect of (1) that most classroom abuse by teachers is likely to occur. This is because of confusion over the role of the teacher in this respect, the extent to which it is reasonable for the teacher to try to enforce their own arbitrary wants, needs, personality traits, or beliefs, and the extent to which a teacher can tolerate or encourage different views from children.

As far as (2) is concerned, a key issue is the balance between learning and teaching. There is no doubt that effective teaching can enhance child learning. However, a very common error is to assume that good child attainment is because of good teaching; many children (and adults) know that good attainment can be in spite of poor teaching. This problem can be more severe in selective schools where children are already known to have high levels of attainment; those high levels of attainment can mask poor or mediocre teaching.

Many classrooms are still based on traditional views of how classes are conducted. Child learning these days is increasingly happening in a complex blended learning environment in which the school is playing a reducing role. There is increasingly urgent need for schools to increase blended learning opportunities for children, and not doing so may render traditional classrooms more dysfunctional to learning, and thus increase the risk of emotional abuse. Groups of bored children are difficult to deal with!

Many readers may think point (3) is somewhat cynical; it isn't. In this increasingly consumerist world, with greater emphasis on self-indulgence and selfishness, and the need for most people to find a job, the developed world has experienced substantial breakdown in community and family. Much of the developing world is going the same way. There is increasing assumption about the need for more stable nuclear families - but that ignores the point that nuclear families are a very modern phenomenon. For thousands of years, humans have been living in extended families or broader communities. There were not the same problems of family isolation from other family or community members who could help with child care. So many families are moving around in pursuit of jobs and careers, leading to substantial community breakdown. As a result, these days, increasing numbers of families are on their own when it comes to child care. Hence schools have an increasing child care role to perform. Just reflect on the number of problems parents may face when a school in the developed world is closed. Many writers suggest a greater need for more 'social capital' (for example, Halpern 2005) and there is extensive debate about this.

As indicated in the Introduction, there are different possible dimensions to the issue of emotional abuse in the classroom:

1. emotional abuse by one child against another child;
2. emotional abuse by a teacher against one or more children;
3. emotional abuse by a one or more children against a teacher.

A term often used for (1) is 'bullying" (although this could also apply to 2 & 3, and bullying can also include physical abuse).

Other terms are important to understand, and have arisen from research into this field.

Indirect and covert aggression are sometimes used for situations where the bullying may not be directly between two specific people. For example, "...spreading rumours, giving someone the silent treatment, or isolating someone from the group..." (Field et al., 2009). This is more likely to occur in situations such as (1) and (3) above, but could also be (2). With this kind of bullying, it is possible for the bully to remain very difficult to detect. Field et al., go on to explain that the terms indirect and covert aggression are also referred to in some literature as relational or social aggression. They point to one interesting trend, that "...girls are more likely to be relationally aggressive than boys...".

For those readers who would like a more international perspective on school bullying, a useful starting point is Smith et al. (1999) who provide a collection of papers about bully research in many different countries. Intriguingly, the index for the book contains no entries that are obvious entries for the terms indirect, covert, relational, or social, with respect to aggression.

It is beyond the scope of this book to go into the research and definitions of these further. In simple terms, relational aggression is concerned with damaging patterns of friendship (i.e. friend relationships); social aggression is intended to damage someone's social status by attacking social or sexual reputation.

The counterpart to indirect or covert aggression is direct or overt. That is the thrust of most literature about bullying (Field et al., 2009; OCC, 2006; Olweus, 1993; Olweus and Limber, 2007; Smith et al., 1999; Volpe, 1980), or school violence (Benbenishty and Astor, 2005), or emotional-psychological abuse (Hyman, 1990; Hyman and Snook, 1999).

One important point coming from the vast majority of the literature, including from well before the UK Elton Report (DES, 1989) is just how pervasive is bullying, and the number of children who have been on the receiving end of some form of bullying.

One more area worth exploring when considering emotional abuse in the classroom, but is something almost completely ignored in the mainstream research and literature about abuse, aggression, and bullying, is educational theory.

The focus of attention is the classroom situation itself. A classroom situation is hundreds, if not thousands, of years old. Of course, until relatively modern times, formal teaching was not accessible to those who had insufficient money. In the UK it took the 1870 Elementary Education Act to start the process of universal free school education. Much of that Act was concerned with the construction of infrastructure for elementary education, leaving the question of attendance to local byelaws.

The generation of information technology concerned with books, printing, paper, binding, and such like, facilitated classroom teaching by easier provision of textbooks and writing books. The latest generation of computer-based information technology is putting increased challenge and stress on the classroom situation. This is because actual child learning is, increasingly, blended learning assisted by modern technology both outside and inside the classroom. Traditional power and status roles between children and teachers are eroding. It is increasingly insufficient for a teacher to insist on respect because of the teacher's position of authority; respect is earned by the teacher by a positive contribution to child learning. Perhaps there is a time lag from changes to traditional manager authority and respect (Darnton and Giacoletto, 1992) to changes in child respect for teachers.

As with other concepts explored in this book, it is beyond its scope to go into depth; the point is to identify key issues.

As children progress through the school system becoming more experienced, methods of learning blend from pedagogy to andragogy, and indeed the research literature probably has too little exploration of the applicability of andragogical theory to children. For example, self-directedness is at the heart of much andragogy writing (Knowles, 1973; Mezirow, 1981). Adult learning is assumed to be more problem-centred, immediately useful or interesting, part of evolving social roles, and more experiential. These are characteristics that are increasingly creeping into child learning environments through the intermediation of new technology and media (although they have been present for many decades in alternative education settings). Therefore, it is likely that the coming years will witness much more of a merging between pedagogy and andragogy. The teacher will evolve into an educator, helping learners to be more self-directed in their learning and its applications in life.

In this brave new educational world, the 'classroom' expands into an environment conducive to learning. The educator is a facilitator, The child is a learner facilitated by the educator.

What may this have to do with emotional abuse in the classroom? There is a risk that as a consequence of greater intermediation of technology and media into a child's learning world, the traditional classroom becomes increasingly dysfunctional with respect to child learning, *and the child knows it because the child becomes aware of how much learning is increasingly taking place outside the classroom.* At its extreme, this means that the traditional classroom itself becomes a more abusive environment if children are forced to remain in such environments; traditional classrooms risk becoming increasingly boring. This, of course, has been recognized by many teachers who are now working hard to integrate new technology and media into the learning environment, increasingly encouraging children to bring their outside learning into the formal learning environment. Traditional teaching, and traditional classroom environments are increasingly under siege.

Having explored several key concepts related to emotional abuse, it is easier to narrow down the scope of this book. In doing so, keep in mind that is in no way diminishing the other forms of abuse or aggression in the classroom. It is because the focus of this book is to put the spotlight on emotional abuse in the classroom.

In terms of the direction of abuse, this book is not going to be concerned further with child bullying of child, or child bullying of teacher; it is concerned with teacher bullying of child.

In terms of punishment, this book is not going to be concerned further with corporal punishment involving pain; it is only concerned with corporal punishment without pain, and non-corporal punishment, when the narrow definition of punishment set out above has ceased to be effective but punishment by way of retaliation or retribution, continues.

In terms of the classroom environment itself, this book is more concerned with more traditional classroom situations, and will not be concerned further with abuse that may arise by virtue of the classroom *per se,* and only where abuse may arise from teacher conduct.

## The Classroom

The previous section touched on several key aspects of aggression and bullying that affect children in and out of the classroom. This book is concerned with in the classroom.

We can have nothing but the greatest respect for a teacher who is able to manage a classroom ecology, ensuring that good learning takes place in what can be a very challenging environment. High levels of professional competence, including self-control, are required.

A classroom is likely to be the most structured environment for child learning. Appropriate order, and what some writers call classroom discipline are required.

When discussing classroom order, it is all too easy to confuse child obedience and child learning. The goal of a well-ordered classroom ecology is to maximize child learning; it is not to maximize child obedience. The greatest risk of child abuse occurring is where a teacher does not have sufficient competence and self-control to maximize child learning and potential. The first element of this is competence as an educator - the teacher may be weak in communicating effectively with children so the children can maximize their learning and potential. One thing a teacher does not want to hear from a child is "that teacher is boring"; of course, that is a much worse statement than "that lesson was boring" - we can all have our off days! - we need to avoid the situation where every day is an 'off day'. The second part of the statement is 'self-control'. Teaching in a classroom is one of those professions that requires a very high minimum standard of self-control.

'Discipline' can be a highly loaded word, and of course it can also be a noun or a verb. Classroom discipline is a subject that has attracted many writers, many of whom have a great deal of experience. As with many other topics in this book, the question of classroom discipline is beyond the book's scope when is comes to carrying out a thorough literature review of the topic; the goal is to provide the reader with useful, pragmatic tools that can be used to identify and avoid teacher abuse in the classroom. McEachern, Aluede and Kenny (2008) make the point that "Classroom discipline is different from emotional abuse perpetrated by teachers"; separating these (classroom discipline and abuse) can be very challenging.

Charles (2002) presents a balanced view of child classroom behaviour summarizing the kinds of behaviour that are inappropriate *in a classroom setting* (recognizing that *some* aspects of the behaviours may be appropriate in other settings): aggression; immorality; defiance; disruption; goofing off (fooling around, out of seat, not doing work set....). His book includes his summaries of several writers on the subject of classroom discipline: Redl and Wattenberg; Skinner; Glasser; Kounin; Ginott; Dreikers; Lee and Marlene Canter; Jones; Albert; Gordon; Nelsen, Lott, and Glenn; Curwin and Mendler; Coloroso; Kyle, Kagan, and Scott; Kohn; and, Charles.

It is likely that a group of teachers discussing these various ideas about classroom discipline would have a lively debate with different people accepting or rejecting ideas, but all the writers have interesting perspectives to think about. Of course, the book offers a very US-centric view of the classroom world, and doubtless there is considerable cultural variation in classroom conduct.

There is a similar debate about factors that improve learning in the classroom (Higgins, Kokotsaki, and Coe, 2011) which could be linked indirectly to emotional abuse in the classroom (although not done explicitly by those authors). This is because their meta analysis identifies effective teacher feedback as giving very high cost benefit (for low cost) along with meta-cognition and self-regulation strategies as high cost benefit for low cost. These are factors helping to create positive school experiences. Presumably, lack of them increases risks to the classroom emotional ecology.

In the modern world with so much modern technology and media intermediating in child learning processes, many parents and teachers worry (understandably) about the possible effects. There is a very interesting discussion of relevant issues in Prensky (2006) who shows how some of the modern technology used by children may enhance learning, rather than inhibit it.

There is certainly a paradigm shift taking place away from respecting teachers because of teacher authority towards respecting teachers because of the contribution a teacher can make towards learning. Modern technology and media are enabling this paradigm shift.

While discussing the intermediation of modern technology, it is interesting to observe and ask if what is happening with social media is a natural response to the recent substantial breakdown in community. As Desmond Morris (1994) observes; "...a similar collapse in a small village produced an immediate response. In the small community, even a stranger is offered aid and treated as a person rather than a non-person. For village-dwellers, the anti-stranger defence mechanism has not been activated...This difference reveals the extent to which the natural tribal urge to cooperate has to be suppressed in the urban environment. As the number of strangers mounts, the helpfulness fades"; is social networking part of building new virtual tribes to replace real tribes? Much more research is needed to explore the extent to which humans do have a tribal instinct, but if true, it would go some way to explaining why it is challenging to create a positive cooperative classroom environment. Most classrooms are part of a modern urban environment. This is one point to keep in mind when considering a classroom ecology, and the extent to which class members are supportive of each other and their learning.

For many teachers, the classroom environment can be a major source of stress; teaching can be an extremely stressful profession.

The pragmatic sections of this book have been derived from the work of Prof. Wayne C. Nesbit of the Memorial University of Newfoundland.

Nesbit (1991) presents a detailed review of much research literature and commentary about teacher stress. This sets the scene for some teachers who are more prone to abuse children in the classroom, as one reaction to the levels of stress. No self-evaluation instrument is included in his book, for teachers to assess their own levels of stress, but a start could be made in constructing such an instrument, from the many references to research and ideas.

Researching actual classroom abuse is problematic, as almost all teachers would be reluctant to participate, if they had been identified as abusing children emotionally, at least some of the time!

In developing the self-evaluation instrument, Nesbit (1991) says: "It is the writer's conviction that most teachers, being genuinely concerned professionals, would be willing to examine their own behaviour if a confidential unobtrusive means were presented for use at their own discretion. In line with this, the Psychological Abuse Scale for Teachers (PAST) was developed".

PAST was developed from research involving "...experienced teachers, university students in teacher training programs, high school students and a small number of related professionals from medicine, psychology and social work".

The data was clustered into subcategories. As Nesbit admits, this yields a definition of emotional abuse, somewhat "iatrogenic"[1].

Notwithstanding the possibility of an iatrogenic definition—the six Ds—it is very powerful and pragmatic when a set of appropriate questions is associated with each of the subcategories.

Of course there is overlap between some of the subcategories. Also, it leaves out physical and sexual abuse, both of which almost certainly include substantial elements of emotional abuse.

The subcategories are set out in Table 1. This table quotes material from Nesbit's book (Nesbit, 1991: 182).

The questions from Nesbit's book have been set out in the Teacher Self-Evaluation chapter of this book.

1 induced

I have 'inverted' Nesbit's PAST questions, and added some more, to produce the questionnaire in the Pupil Self-Evaluation Chapter. The Pupil Self-Evaluation Questions are new, and entirely my responsibility.

It is hoped that many of these self-evaluation questionnaires will be completed and sent to the author so that a profile can be constructed. Readers are invited to visit the website:

http://ClassroomEmotionalAbuse.com/

to complete the online questionnaire there, and provide examples of good and poor practice.

Following on from the research that developed PAST, Nesbit and Philpott (2002) report the development of a Scale of Subtle Emotional Abuse (SSEA). That scale has 32 items clustered in seven broad areas: body language; discrimination; grading practices; time utilization; treatment of exceptional children; verbal interactions/questioning techniques, and, random behaviour.

Following on from this first edition of this book, it is hoped that there will also be feedback from teachers so that the next edition can have a discussion of pupil abuse of teachers. Ideally, that would also be accompanied by a 'reflected' set of questions for pupils about their conduct towards teachers.

| **Subcategory** | **Explanation** |
|---|---|
| Demeaning | behaviours which humiliate, denigrate and lower self-esteem through embarrassment and verbal belittling |
| Discriminating | behaviours which are prejudicial or biased against specific individuals or groups based upon sex, race, socioeconomic level, cognitive ability or other such factors |
| Dominating | behaviours which sharply define parameters for interaction and control, limit, and/or stifle growth in competence, confidence and independent thought |
| Destabilizing | behaviours which intimidate or induce anxiety, fear and tension |

| Subcategory | Explanation |
|---|---|
| Distancing | behaviours which indicate rejection, isolation and lack of emotional support. Fostering insecurity through insensitivity to feelings and disregard for emotional needs. |
| Diverse | behaviours related to teacher attitude and decorum which negatively influence the classroom ambience |

**Table 1 - Emotional Abuse - Nesbit's Behavioural Subcategories**

# Child Protection, Safeguarding and Safer Recruitment

## Child Protection

Firstly, we will continue to look at the issue of punishment. The relationship between punishment and child protection is not as straight-forward as it may seem. There is unending debate whether punishment is necessary for protection, or if protection implies no punishment.

In practice, virtually all cultures practice forms of punishment, whether for children or adults.

As far as children are concerned, many people hold strong beliefs, which may be supported by religion, that child protection *requires* that children are punished sometimes, including physical punishment with pain. ("spare the rod; spoil the child"). In other words, they believe that sometimes *not* punishing children for misbehaviour would be child abuse. In contrast, as is well known, many people believe the opposite: punishing children is child abuse. For example, there is a discussion about discipline issues in both Christianity and the Quran in CDD (2011).

Research about the outcomes of child physical punishment with pain is somewhat inconclusive, largely because of difficulties, or even muddle, in exploring related variables when researching child outcomes from various kinds of punishment.

As mentioned in the Introduction, one interesting historical irony is that in the UK, the cane was introduced in part as a child protection measure (hard to believe these days) - child protection against sexual abuse that may be involved in teachers spanking bare bottoms!

Therefore, in many parts of the UK, the cane became the punishment device of choice for most teachers who delivered corporal punishment, when they were prohibited from requiring children to remove all their clothing. In a smaller number of schools, the tawse was the punishment device of choice, usually applied to the hand rather than the bottom - the hand is very sensitive.

All this suggests that when considering punishment in a child protection context it is necessary to give primary importance to the effect on the child.

Putting on one side the possible complexities of the person inflicting a punishment, such as sadism or eroticism, it is the effect on the child that is of primary importance. If the child senses that the punishment being received is providing some kind of gratification to the punisher, it is much more likely that the effect on the child is abusive.

Generally, children know if they have behaved in a way that is likely to attract punishment. A child is likely to be acutely aware whether a punishment is being inflicted because of a very specific misbehaviour, or because it is a mode of expression of the punisher.

Thus, we must conclude that sometimes punishment is not abusive in the generally understood meaning of the term, and in some cases it is.

Moving on from punishment, child protection has a much wider remit.

Punishment may or may not be abusive. Most people will agree that violence without any pretence of punishment almost certainly is abuse (there may be remote exceptions, such as physical intervention to prevent violence - 'violence' to stop violence).

Child protection is merging into 'safeguarding', and any distinction between these is becoming increasingly blurred.

Traditionally, child protection is concerned with a few distinct problems:

- child physical abuse
- child sexual abuse
- child neglect
- child psychological abuse

Given the merging of the debate between these, to keep some space between them, it is probably appropriate to say that child protection includes all the infrastructure and mechanisms to deal with them, whereas Safeguarding is more to do with prevention. I know some will not want this distinction.

The approach to child protection in the UK (and in other countries also) had emerged as a multi-agency issue ranging from law enforcement to social welfare and education. Policy formulation has lurched from one high profile case to another, frequently adjusting agency and inter-agency roles to try to plug gaps that led to the latest high profile case. There has been an almost total absence of holistic evidence based policy formulation focussed on the needs and rights of the child. Even the debate on educational institutions is often narrowly focussed on the economic needs of the nation rather than the holistic development of the children; children must be efficient for employers.

As far as schools are concerned, physical punishment is controlled or forbidden in many jurisdictions, but still permitted in many. As school are not generally concerned with the maintenance of children, child neglect is an extremely uncommon issue for schools (other than observing or detecting it). That leaves sexual and psychological abuse that can be problems within schools themselves. There are certainly media reported cases of sexual abuse in schools from time to time. There is much less about psychological abuse - hence one reason for this book - explore the issue in more detail.

An important child protection measure for schools is the extent to which children feel happy and safe in a particular school. According to a great deal of research, the most likely reasons contributing to children not feeling safe are bullying and psychological abuse, both of which can be disturbingly common, and have a devastating impact on a child.

## Safeguarding

Safeguarding, in general, is intimately related to child protection. Indeed, one very helpful book about child protection (Wilson and James, 2007) - called 'The Child Protection Handbook' - is subtitled 'the practitioner's guide to safeguarding children'.

In schools, the question of safeguarding is usually dealt with by increasing awareness of the issues, detecting possible problems for further referral, liaising with other agencies when necessary, and preventative measures for child protection.

It is a key theme of this book, that a general weakness in school safeguarding concerns emotional abuse in the classroom by teachers. That is something within the control of school management. There is a distinct lack of material for school stakeholders to understand what constitutes emotional abuse, detecting it, and managing it. Teachers have very little supporting material to help them with their professional development in this field, hence the pragmatic approach in this book, of providing a teacher self-diagnostic tool.

There is a UK government publication setting out an official position on safeguarding in schools. (DfES 2007a). Keeping track of UK government publications and responsibilities is not helped by frequent departmental renaming and reformation by breaking up and forming different combinations of responsibilities, accompanied by removing websites, some of which are archived, and some which are not. Often, trying to follow URLs on recent government publications yields a 'not found' result without appropriate forwarding or signposting being put in place. Some politicians must relish spending substantial sums of taxpayer money on departmental re-branding and reforming, burying key publications in the process! This document (DfES, 2007a) is statutory guidance. Notwithstanding that, neither of the key URLs on the publication works (July 2012) or redirects to its current location. Finding it on the new Department for Education website requires less obvious searches. Having found its current location, the back page has not been updated to provide current correct signposting. So much for government rhetoric about child safeguarding being of primary importance! Of course, school stakeholders cannot use ignorance of the law as an excuse for any failings even if the location of statements of the law has been obscured. It will probably take another serious case inquiry to observe the difficulty of obtaining the statutory guidance, and make a recommendation for the guidance to be more clearly available, and updated with accurate signposting information.

The nearest that the statutory guidance gets to a definition of safeguarding is probably its 'Shared Objectives':

"1.1. Everyone in the education service shares an objective to help keep children and young people safe by contributing to:

- providing a safe environment for children and young people to learn in education settings; and
- identifying children and young people who are suffering or likely to suffer significant harm, and taking appropriate action with the aim of making sure they are kept safe both at home and in the education setting."

The scope of the statutory guidance is identified by suggestions of what needs to be done.

"1.2. Achieving this objective requires systems designed to:

- prevent unsuitable people working with children and young people;
- promote safe practice and challenge poor and unsafe practice;
- identify instances in which there are grounds for concern about a child's welfare, and initiate or take appropriate action to keep them safe; and
- contribute to effective partnership working between all those involved with providing services for children and young people."

As will be seen in the next chapter, this statutory guidance falls far short of the aspirations set out in the UK Every Child Matters agenda.

For example, 1.1 only refers to 'significant harm'. As seen earlier, that is a term over the legal threshold for state intervention. A child with a very unhappy school experience is likely to have been harmed even if the harm did not reach the current statutory threshold for intervention.

These statutory guidelines do mention the Children Act 2004, but primarily concerned with local authorities' arrangements for child protection. Well-being (the basis for Every Child Matters) is mentioned in passing.

These guidelines are more focussed on child protection, and recommendations arising from previous serious cases, than focussed on the education of the child.

The classroom teacher is not going to get much help from these guidelines, other than meeting a statutory requirement to be familiar with their provisions. The teacher must look elsewhere for help about what child 'wellbeing' is really about. In other words, these guidelines are important when considering significant harm; they are not helpful when considering 'harm'.

It is for reasons like this, that the matter of emotional abuse in the classroom has 'slipped through the net'.

The classroom teacher will find more assistance from another UK government publication about safeguarding (DCSF, 2010). That publication is not statutory guidance as is DfES (2007a). However, in addition to problems following URLs on DfES (2007a), DCSF (2010) is also no longer available in its hardcopy form! (July 2012).

The definition of emotional abuse from that publication (DCSF, 2010) has already been given earlier in the discussion about "what is emotional abuse?". The same publication goes further, in a way that explains why emotional abuse can have serious, long-lasting effects: "There is increasing evidence of the adverse long-term consequences for children's development where they have been subject to sustained emotional abuse, including the impact of serious bullying. Emotional abuse has an important impact on a developing child's mental health, behaviour and self-esteem. It can be especially damaging in infancy. Underlying emotional abuse may be as important, if not more so, as other more visible forms of abuse in terms of its impact on the child. Domestic violence is abusive in itself. Adult mental health problems and parental substance misuse may be features in families where children are exposed to such abuse".

Although that quotation is not specifically addressed at teacher emotional abuse in the classroom, it is highly relevant because of the potential long-term impact on a child's view of the school, and a child's overall enjoyment of school. Of course, different children will react differently, but careless treatment of children at school by teachers can have a long-lasting damaging effect on children.

In terms of safeguarding, it is now a statutory duty to be concerned about "physical and mental health and emotional well-being" of children, whether in or out of the school environment.

However, the law is very muddled about where that statutory duty lies. The Children Act 2004 places such a duty on children's services authorities which include a range of 'relevant partners'. Astonishingly, schools are not included as 'relevant partners'.

Children's service authorities "must have regard to the importance of parents and other persons caring for children in improving the well-being of children". Thus, schools are brought into the ambit of the work of the authorities, even though not formally 'relevant partners'.

Thus, it can be safely assumed that the matter of the emotional well-being of the classroom child, and the avoidance of emotional abuse, are not only professional duties, but also statutory duties in the UK.

The people most likely to know if there is a possibility of abuse having taken place, are the children themselves; something has happened in the classroom that has made them distinctly uncomfortable.

Of course, there are some forms of abuse where the child may

The safer recruitment procedures came out of another serious case review, reacting to the horrific murders of Jessica Chapman and Holly Wells by a person who had been hired by a school, notwithstanding his previous and known criminal history.

The procedures advised, apply to "...everyone who works in an education setting where there are children under 18 who is likely to be perceived by the children as a safe and trustworthy adult".

Thus it is not only for teachers; it is for everyone likely to come into contact with children in an educational setting, paid or unpaid.

The guidelines go on to discuss a number of relevant matters, such as: preliminary checks; statements about recruitment and selection policies; advertising; application forms; job descriptions; references; short-listing; interviews; and, appointments. They go further than recruitment and selection, giving advice also on handling allegations against staff.

A teacher recruitment panel must have someone who holds a certificate of having passed a safer recruitment test.

As with so many procedures related to safeguarding, for the purposes of this book, a key weakness lies in the absence of evidence-based checks for problems such as emotional abuse. It is very easy for an emotionally abusive teacher to get through the current safeguarding and safer recruitment procedures. When that happens, the subsequent impact on children can be serious and long-lasting.

# Every Child Matters

At the time of writing this book, the overall UK framework covering matters of child welfare is referred to as Every Child Matters (ECM).

ECM was another major government initiative triggered by yet another tragic child death in circumstances of serious abuse that occurred after some state agencies became aware there were problems for the child, but without effective intervention.

ECM is at a minimum a really admirable example of political rhetoric suggesting solutions to a very wide range of problems. It is admirable because of its very wide scope, and clear articulation of several fundamental issues that are undoubtedly important for child welfare. It is rhetoric because actual steps taken following the publication of ECM and the enactment of the Children Act 2004 fall far short of the admirable ECM promises.

ECM started life as a government green paper (DfES 2003b). Following the green paper, the government published its responses to the consultation, and next steps (DfES 2004b). After the Children Act 2004, the government issued another publication summarizing the essence of ECM and setting out concrete implementation steps (DfES 2004a).

The admirable scope of ECM covers 5 principal outcomes:

- Be healthy
- Stay safe
- Enjoy and achieve
- Make a positive contribution
- Achieve economic well-being

There are 25 specific 'aims' included in these outcomes. (see Table 5.1). Very few people are likely to reject the aims set out in ECM, and if only they could be realized.

The problems with ECM are more to do with omission, than commission, and the overall thrust of ECM. Some of these omissions are linked intimately with problems of emotional abuse in the classroom.

| Outcome | Aims |
| --- | --- |
| Be healthy | • Physically healthy<br>• Mentally and emotionally healthy<br>• Sexually healthy<br>• Healthy lifestyles<br>• Choose not to take illegal drugs<br>*Parents, carers and families promote healthy choices* |
| Stay safe | • Safe from maltreatment, neglect, violence and sexual exploitation<br>• Safe from accidental injury and death<br>• Safe from bullying and discrimination<br>• Safe from crime and anti-social behaviour in and out of school<br>• Have security, stability and are cared for<br>*Parents, carers and families provide safe homes and stability* |
| Enjoy and achieve | • Ready for school<br>• Attend and enjoy school<br>• Achieve stretching national educational standards at primary school<br>• Achieve personal and social development and enjoy recreation<br>• Achieve stretching national educational standards at secondary school<br>*Parents, carers and families support learning* |
| Make a positive contribution | • Engage in decision-making and support the community and environment<br>• Engage in law-abiding and positive behaviour in and out of school<br>• Develop positive relationships and choose not to bully and discriminate<br>• Develop self-confidence and successfully deal with significant life changes and challenges<br>• Develop enterprising behaviour<br>*Parents, carers and families promote positive behaviour* |
| Achieve economic well-being | • Engage in further education, employment or training on leaving school<br>• Ready for employment<br>• Live in decent homes and sustainable communities<br>• Access to transport and material goods<br>• Live in households free from low income<br>*Parents, carers and families are supported to be economically active* |

**Table 5.1 Every Child Matters - Outcomes and Aims**

It is worthwhile taking a brief look at the background to ECM.

There are absolutely clear links between the very unfortunate case of Victoria Climbié and ECM; almost all writers make this connection - it should be assumed to be explicit. If there is any sense of equivocation in those words, it is because of the background prior to the Victoria Climbié case, and that case proved to be a catalyst to bring together concerns about a range of issues much wider than those involved specifically in the case.

The Victoria Climbié case is very difficult to comprehend. The circumstances of her death make extremely difficult reading. The institutional failures will be incomprehensible to most people, as indeed they were difficult to comprehend by the Inquiry chairman himself (Laming, 2003). There have been numerous studies of this case looking at the institutional problems in more detail (for example, White, 2009).

The Laming Report has 108 recommendations; 'every child matters' is not one of them. The term was introduced by the Government response to the Laming Report (DfES, 2003a) as the title of its accompanying green paper (DfES, 2003b).

The Laming Report needs to be put into context. It followed in excess of 70 official reports from the previous decades about similar issues and "the many public inquiries over the previous thirty years" (Parton, 2004)[1]. If it took more than 70 previous official reports, plus the Laming Report, before ECM the government has not been able to deal with the issues raised in all of those reports. The critiques of ECM show that there is still a long way to go. Parton (2011) has an interesting summary of the page counts of various government reports for 1974-2010. The data he presents is shown in Figure 5.1 (at the end of the chapter). Lord Laming was surprised how so many agencies and professionals were capable of such lamentable failures as led to the death of Victoria Climbié; of course, they didn't kill her - that was down to the people convicted of her murder - but they didn't do what was needed to prevent it.

As will be seen when the weaknesses in ECM are discussed, there are still elements of the Laming Report that have not yet been addressed. Why not? - government hesitation - and some of that hesitation explains why the safeguarding problems of sexual abuse, and emotional abuse in the classroom, remain.

The five outcomes (set out in Table 5.1) emerge in the green

1 There is lots about such inquiries, e.g: Hopkins (2007), Parton (2011), Wilson and James (2007).

paper "When we consulted children, young people and families, they wanted the Government to set out a positive vision of the outcomes we want to achieve. The five outcomes which mattered most to children and young people were:

- **being healthy:** enjoying good physical and mental health and living a healthy lifestyle
- **staying safe:** being protected from harm and neglect
- **enjoying and achieving:** getting the most out of life and developing the skills for adulthood
- **making a positive contribution:** being involved with the community and society and not engaging in anti-social or offending behaviour
- **economic well-being:** not being prevented by economic disadvantage from achieving their full potential in life."

Although not presenting actual data, here the government green paper is saying that these outcomes are a summary of the results of people they consulted.

These outcomes take the green paper far beyond the original recommendations of the Laming Report (DfES, 2003b) arising from the Victoria Climbié case, but many of the Report recommendations do find their way into the green paper; some don't.

These five outcomes eventually emerged from the green paper consultation process as statutory provisions in the Children Act 2004.

At a national level, the Act establishes the Children's Commissioner in Part 1, with general functions that include:

**"2 General functions**

2 (3)The Children's Commissioner is to be concerned in particular under this section with the views and interests of children so far as relating to the following aspects of their well-being—

(a) physical and mental health and emotional well-being;

(b) protection from harm and neglect;

(c) education, training and recreation;

(d) the contribution made by them to society;

(e) social and economic well-being."

Part two of the Act sets out responsibilities for children's services authorities, including those five outcomes:

**"10 Co-operation to improve well-being**

(2)The arrangements are to be made with a view to improving the well-being of children in the authority's area so far as relating to—

(a) physical and mental health and emotional well-being;
(b) protection from harm and neglect;
(c) education, training and recreation;
(d) the contribution made by them to society;
(e) social and economic well-being."

In case any reader is puzzled about what is a 'children's services authority'in today's grand scheme of government activities, there were important changes to the concepts of 'children's services authority' and 'local education authority' by 'The Local Education Authorities and Children's Services Authorities (Integration of Functions) Order 2010'. For many readers, the change from 'local education authority' to 'local authority' is likely to be surprising because the term 'local education authority' (LEA) is still in widespread use.

As pointed out earlier, it is somewhat surprising that schools are not included in the list of 'relevant partners' of a children's services authority[2]. Schools would be involved via a catch-all in the Act: "10 (3) In making arrangements under this section a children's services authority in England must have regard to the importance of parents and other persons caring for children in improving the well-being of children".

Interestingly, the children's services authorities don't have to take into account the views of children, but the Children's Commissioner does:

" 2 (4) The Children's Commissioner must take reasonable steps to involve children in the discharge of his function under this section, and in particular to—

(a) ensure that children are made aware of his function and how they may communicate with him; and

(b) consult children, and organisations working with children, on the matters he proposes to consider or research under subsection (2) (c) or (d).

(5) Where the Children's Commissioner publishes a report

2 [who are: county council (including any district councils); police authority and the chief officer of police for a police area any part of which falls within the area of the children's services authority; a local probation board for an area any part of which falls within the area of the authority; a youth offending team for an area any part of which falls within the area of the authority; a Strategic Health Authority and Primary Care Trust for an area any part of which falls within the area of the authority; a person providing services under section 114 of the Learning and Skills Act 2000 (c. 21) in any part of the area of the authority; the Learning and Skills Council for England.]

under this section he must, if and to the extent that he considers it appropriate, also publish the report in a version which is suitable for children (or, if the report relates to a particular group of children, for those children)."

So, children should be involved in some of the work of the Commissioner, and within certain constraints, make reports intelligible to children.

It would be very interesting to see the results of research into child awareness of the work of the Children's Commissioner.

As far as this book is concerned, the need to explore the question of classroom emotional abuse would seem to be a perfectly legitimate research area for the Commissioner (this is enabled by s2(2)(c) of the Act).

Schools should ensure that their safeguarding training includes references to the work of the Commissioner, and it would also be a very good idea for schools to ensure that their PSHE (Personal, Social, and Health Education) curriculum also includes learning about the Commissioner and the work of the Commissioner.

Although not included in the government's white paper, the Children's Commissioner works with a remit that includes "promotes and protects children's rights under the United Nations Convention on the Rights of the Child (UNCRC) ratified by the UK in 1991. Our energies focus especially on both policy and practice where children's rights are ignored or violated" (OCC, 2012).

## Critical Perspectives on ECM and Safeguarding

There is, obviously, substantial government policy related to matters of child protection and safeguarding, culminating in the current multi-faceted Every Child Matters.

In some cases, it is necessary to learn specific material in order to obtain accreditation or certification for certain statutorily influenced matters, such as attendance at safeguarding training, or obtaining safer recruitment certification.

Government policy is not entirely ideological, and some of it is underpinned with an evidence base. Having said that, ECM and safeguarding are not without their critics, and some of the criticism is soundly based.

ECM is somewhat at odds with the Education Acts because it refers to school rather than education or learning, ignoring the legal requirement for full-time education by attendance at school *or otherwise*. As will be seen later, the United Nations Convention on the rights of the Child places emphasis on education rather than school.

One book that is a resource just about everyone concerned with safeguarding should read, is that edited by Broadhurst, Grover, and Jamieson (2009a), even if only the introduction (Broadhurst, Grover, and Jamieson, 2009b). Anyone who wishes to exercise critical thinking (and that should include all students and lecturers) needs access to sources of material that do take a critical (or challenging) view of much orthodox wisdom.

Perhaps the key problem with the orthodox approaches to safeguarding, is the set of deeply ingrained cultural prejudices that can underpin so many expectations. For example: "These observations are important because they demonstrate that resistance to inclusion in services is not born out of deviancy or pathological failings. The observations suggest that it is the ways in which educational institutions are embedded in a deeply socially and culturally unequal society that is the problem for the 'hard to reach', rather than the 'hard to reach' being the problem" (Warin 2009, p139).

Warin's comments follow some summary comments bringing together multiple research notes: "Relevant here are findings from studies...that reveal that a lack of so-called help-seeking behaviour may be explained by a resistance to the perceived values of UK liberalism... 'an excessive individualism and materialism, in which personal gratification and fulfilment undermine more family-oriented values'...These studies suggest that parents in these families are likely to feel they have little to learn about parenting from the UK's educational establishments...".

It is not the job of this book to repeat these summaries of studies, but to make the point that every professional with responsibility for safeguarding should take the time to read perspectives that are radically different from the social and cultural assumptions implicit in programmes such as ECM and safeguarding; we can add inclusiveness to the list of substantial problems (sexual abuse, and teacher abuse in the classroom). that remain to be addressed comprehensively.

Warin's observations are important not only for cross-cultural understanding, but also for understanding different 'sub-cultures'.

Those who think that progress is being made in the UK following the institutionalization of ECM and the Children Act 2004, will find some UNICEF observations very sober reading.

In the now famous (infamous?) UNICEF Report Card for 2007, the UK was placed at the bottom of the league for the average score of dimensions of well-being. It was also bottom for 2 of the 6 dimensions: family and peer relationships; behaviours and risks (UNICEF 2007, p2).

In a later report by UNICEF, the unanimous suggestion from children was simplicity itself: "The message from all the children who participated in the research was simple, clear and unanimous: their well-being centres on time with a happy family whose interactions are consistent and secure; having good friends; and having plenty of things to do, especially outdoors" (UNICEF 2011, p.2).

In a useful triangulation when considered alongside some of the points made by Warin, the UNICEF report also observes: "In the comparison of children's and families' experiences in the UK, Spain and Sweden, we found that a materialistic and commercial culture is embedded in the UK and in concepts of good parenting in a way that is not seen in Spain and Sweden" (UNICEF 2011, p6).

The UNICEF had commented that some progress had been made since 2007, but this is now likely to go into reverse with current government policies. One of its reports has some sober advice: "The Government must now show strong leadership in order to support families to fight back against the ways in which the UK's materialistic culture embeds inequality in our society, affects family time and relationships, and has a negative impact on children's well-being." (UNICEF 2011, p7).

In terms of child abuse, these points raise some extremely difficult and intransigent issues and challenges to ensure that classroom demands for child compliance are not based on such fundamentally problematic social and cultural trends. Clearly there are major issues raised for the PSHE curriculum.

The current policy focus on *individual* responsibility, whether child or parent, fails to acknowledge, let alone deal with, the deeper social and cultural issues that are undermining child happiness and welfare. Reorganization of children services may go part of the way, but does not even begin to touch on the more fundamental issues affecting child welfare. This is discussed in part by Broadhurst (2009) while discussing the government initiative *Every Parent Matters* (DfES 2007b). One great danger of much government policy is to see child problems as a matter *within families,* rather than exploring the effects of socioeconomic norms and rhetoric. Keep in mind that the nuclear family is a very recent innovation, with successive governments being content to see the destruction of community and other wider mechanisms beyond nuclear families. State intervention and control is not a substitute for real community; nor are neo-liberal concepts of free market forces along with keeping down wages and welfare costs. UNICEF report frequently about child poverty (e.g., UNICEF, 2012).

Does 'every child matter' - even in the ECM sense of the term? - well, not if you are the child of an asylum seeker or certain immigrants.

Obviously, there are major debates to be had about this, but punish the children? So ECM applies to all children; some more equally than others (Grover, 2009).

There has certainly not been a shortage of government initiatives: "The National Childcare Strategy, Quality Protects, Sure Start, the Children's Fund, Choice Protects, Youth Inclusion and Support Panels, Every Child Matters, Multi-Agency Panels, Championing Children, the Children's Workforce Development Council, National Service Frameworks and National Standards, the Children's Plan—these are just some of the child welfare/safeguarding initiatives..." (Taylor 2009, p30). Most professionals in the field will be able to add a few more.

One could be forgiven for thinking that all of these initiatives are evidence of a serious lack of joined-up thinking about child welfare, with approaches that are skirting round the really serious issue, or the initiatives arise because of a '2nd corollary to the history repeats itself saying' (history repeats itself; 1st corollary - those who don't learn from history, end up repeating it; 2nd corollary - it may have been done before but I haven't done it yet). Maybe too many people have the power and resources to start something without having to discuss with others, and without having to produce evidence.

Although ECM is often put forward as a program with a focus on the welfare of the child, there are other changes that have also increased the risks of children being criminalized (Fitzpatrick, 2009; Jamieson, 2009).

Other important debates around ECM include government policy concerning young people and alcohol and drugs (Paylor, 2009), health (Peckover, 2009) and the Common Assessment Framework itself (Pithouse and Broadhurst, 2009) used in the management of some safeguarding issues.

The UN Declaration on the Rights of the Child (UNDRC) in 1959, set out in Appendix C, provides an international anchor for child rights. That followed a very short and simple League of Nations document from 1924.

Some 30 years later in 1989 there was a Convention (UNGA 1989 - see Appendic C)) on the rights of the child (UNCRC). The Convention has not been brought into UK law, in the same way that the European Convention on Human Rights has, even though it has been ratified by the UK, albeit initially with certain reservations, subsequently removed after many years of battling by various agencies and social workers. A key motive for the reservations was the way children of asylum seekers and immigrants may be treated by UK authorities. Several other European countries have brought the UNCRC into domestic law.

ECM and UNCRC do not sit together very comfortably. There is a helpful discussion about this in Archard (2009). While commending several features of ECM, Archard goes on to say: "There is thus no appreciation of the possibility that children might have rights as children. Most striking is the fact that ECM contains not a single reference to the UNCRC, not even an acknowledgement that the UK has ratified the Convention" (Archard, 2009, p42).

On an initial investigation, Archard may appear to be somewhat harsh. However, in its response to the Victoria Climbié Inquiry Report, Recommendation 3, to consider the implementation of the UNCRC and explore its implementation, the government was completely silent and simply didn't address it, either by accepting or rejecting - it was as though that part of the recommendation didn't exist! Eventually, the Children's Commissioner explicitly uses the UNCRC to guide her work: "The Commissioner uses the United Nations Convention on the Rights of the Child (UNCRC) to guide her work" (OCC 2010).

However, Archard's key point remains: the UK, for various reasons, has not imported UNCRC into UK domestic law, and certainly seems completely unwilling to accept anything such as children rights, notwithstanding its ratification of the UNCRC.

The stark reality for the UK government is that it is under a legal obligation to deliver those child rights, even if it does mean taking steps to eliminate child poverty and its consequences for child development: "By agreeing to undertake the obligations of the Convention (by ratifying or acceding to it), national governments have committed themselves to protecting and ensuring children's rights and they have agreed to hold themselves accountable for this commitment before the international community. States parties to the Convention are obliged to develop and undertake all actions and policies in the light of the best interests of the child" (UNGA 1989).

The last thing the government would want to see in place is legislation by which it could be called to book for its tardiness.

The interested reader is referred to Archard (2009) for further information about UK extreme reluctance to see its UNCRC obligations written into UK domestic law, and to Hill and Hopkins (2009) for further information about the UK approach to child asylum seekers, either unaccompanied or as family members.

Until UK equivocation about the UNCRC is rectified, ECM is rendered seriously 'wounded'.

Whatever the UK government's equivocation, it is bound by Article 2 which prohibits any form of discrimination against children, and Article 22 that covers children seeking refugee status. Therefore, there is a strong likelihood that some of its treatment of children from asylum and immigrant children is simply unlawful. If the government can't accept its own legal obligations, it is not setting a particularly good example for others. However, that doesn't excuse others.

Using the UNCRC in legal proceedings is tedious, and sometimes will fail, because the use must be indirect, often using the Human Rights Act as a vehicle to use the UNCRC for purposes of interpretation.

The advice to the classroom teacher can only be to study the UNCRC, and for each individual to act as far as possible to supplement ECM with the rights rendered by the Convention given the UK's obligations. It is highly likely that this will enhance teacher acceptance by pupils.

This book advises Schools to develop a Children Rights Policy. *As far as the classroom is concerned*, there are some rights that have direct applicability, as shown in Table 5.2.

It should be noted that many of the rights conveyed to children are not absolute rights, and in many parts of the Convention, the rights of a particular child are balanced against the rights of others. So, for example, as far as rights of expression are concerned, there are important balances: "The exercise of this right may be subject to certain restrictions, but these shall only be such as are provided by law and are necessary: ... (a) For respect of the rights or reputations of others; or..." (Article 13). Where this is such a balancing of the rights of the individual child with the rights of others, that is indicated in Table 5.2 by a 'Q' (for 'qualified') following the Article number.

The common simple expedient used by many states in respect of internationally agreed obligations, is to work towards having international treaties and conventions have written in, recognition of an individual state's own laws.

The UNCRC has many articles which recognize the laws of sovereign states, but this is a qualified recognition, with many Articles having an expression such as "...provided by law and are necessary...". It is the 'and' followed by 'are necessary'; it is insufficient that a possible deviation from the Convention is 'provided by law'; it must also be 'necessary'. Many states have many laws that are not 'necessary' (including the UK) for the proper functioning of a variety of rights and obligations, they are often the result of some political or economic pressure group succeeding in procuring the law to favour their desired position; the law can be a very powerful political tool, particularly in the absence of a written constitution.

| Article | Text | Effect |
|---|---|---|
| 12 | States Parties shall assure to the child who is capable of forming his or her own views the right to express those views freely in all matters affecting the child, the views of the child being given due weight in accordance with the age and maturity of the child. | Freedom of expression |
| 13<br>Q | The child shall have the right to freedom of expression; this right shall include freedom to seek, receive and impart information and ideas of all kinds, regardless of frontiers, either orally, in writing or in print, in the form of art, or through any other media of the child's choice. | Freedom of expression |

| Article | Text | Effect |
|---|---|---|
| 14<br>Q | States Parties shall respect the right of the child to freedom of thought, conscience and religion. | Freedom of thought, conscience and religion. |
| 15<br>Q | States Parties recognize the rights of the child to freedom of association and to freedom of peaceful assembly. | Rights of assembly and association. |
| 16 | No child shall be subjected to arbitrary or unlawful interference with his or her privacy, family, home or correspondence, nor to unlawful attacks on his or her honour and reputation. | Rights of privacy, family life, and reputation. |
| 19(1) | 1. States Parties shall take all appropriate legislative, administrative, social and educational measures to protect the child from all forms of physical or mental violence, injury or abuse, neglect or negligent treatment, maltreatment or exploitation, including sexual abuse, while in the care of parent(s), legal guardian(s) or any other person who has the care of the child. | Child protection and Safeguarding |
| 19(2) | 2. Such protective measures should, as appropriate, include effective procedures for the establishment of social programmes to provide necessary support for the child and for those who have the care of the child, as well as for other forms of prevention and for identification, reporting, referral, investigation, treatment and follow-up of instances of child maltreatment described heretofore, and, as appropriate, for judicial involvement. | Child protection and Safeguarding |
| 20 | A child temporarily or permanently deprived of his or her family environment, or in whose own best interests cannot be allowed to remain in that environment, shall be entitled to special protection and assistance provided by the State. | Looked After Children |

| Article | Text | Effect |
|---|---|---|
| 23 | States Parties recognize that a mentally or physically disabled child should enjoy a full and decent life, in conditions which ensure dignity, promote self-reliance and facilitate the child's active participation in the community. | SEN - Special Educational Needs |
| 28 (1) (a)-(b) | 1. States Parties recognize the right of the child to education, and with a view to achieving this right progressively and on the basis of equal opportunity, they shall, in particular:<br>(a) Make primary education compulsory and available free to all;<br>(b) Encourage the development of different forms of secondary education, including general and vocational education, make them available and accessible to every child, and take appropriate measures such as the introduction of free education and offering financial assistance in case of need; | Education Rights |
| 28 (1) (c)-(e) | (c) Make higher education accessible to all on the basis of capacity by every appropriate means;<br>(d) Make educational and vocational information and guidance available and accessible to all children;<br>(e) Take measures to encourage regular attendance at schools and the reduction of drop-out rates. | Education Rights |
| 28(2) | 2. States Parties shall take all appropriate measures to ensure that school discipline is administered in a manner consistent with the child's human dignity and in conformity with the present Convention. | Education Rights |

| Article | Text | Effect |
|---|---|---|
| 29(1) (a)-(b) | 1. States Parties agree that the education of the child shall be directed to: (a) The development of the child's personality, talents and mental and physical abilities to their fullest potential; (b) The development of respect for human rights and fundamental freedoms, and for the principles enshrined in the Charter of the United Nations; | Education Rights |
| 29(1) (c) | (c) The development of respect for the child's parents, his or her own cultural identity, language and values, for the national values of the country in which the child is living, the country from which he or she may originate, and for civilizations different from his or her own; | Education Rights |
| 29(1) (d)-(e) | (d) The preparation of the child for responsible life in a free society, in the spirit of understanding, peace, tolerance, equality of sexes, and friendship among all peoples, ethnic, national and religious groups and persons of indigenous origin; (e) The development of respect for the natural environment. | Education Rights |
| 31 | 1. States Parties recognize the right of the child to rest and leisure, to engage in play and recreational activities appropriate to the age of the child and to participate freely in cultural life and the arts. | Right to cultural etc., participation |
| 32 | 1. States Parties recognize the right of the child to be protected from economic exploitation and from performing any work that is likely to be hazardous or to interfere with the child's education, or to be harmful to the child's health or physical, mental, spiritual, moral or social development. | Right to freedom from economic etc. exploitation |

| Article | Text | Effect |
|---|---|---|
| 34 | States Parties undertake to protect the child from all forms of sexual exploitation and sexual abuse. For these purposes, States Parties shall in particular take all appropriate national, bilateral and multilateral measures to prevent: (a) The inducement or coercion of a child to engage in any unlawful sexual activity; | Right to freedom from sexual exploitation |
| 37(d) | States Parties shall ensure that: (d) Every child deprived of his or her liberty shall have the right to prompt access to legal and other appropriate assistance, as well as the right to challenge the legality of the deprivation of his or her liberty before a court or other competent, independent and impartial authority, and to a prompt decision on any such action. | Right to challenge detentions |
| 42 | States Parties undertake to make the principles and provisions of the Convention widely known, by appropriate and active means, to adults and children alike. | Knowledge of UNCRC |

**Table 5.2 United Nations Convention on the Rights of the Child - Articles applicable to classroom activity.**

## Children Rights Policy for Schools

When looking at these child rights, accepted by the UK, the impact on the school is to suggest that a Policy would be very helpful to demonstrate how the school uses the UNCRC to supplement its policies for child protection, safeguarding, and ECM. A template Policy is suggested in Appendix C An alternative (or additional) approach by a school, would be to add supplementary material to an existing policy, or even to extend relevant policies with acknowledgement of, and an indication of how the relevant UNCRC articles are handled in each specific policy. Some policies overlap with broader safeguarding requirements. A common weakness in school policies concerns looked after children. Reports to governors are common. Those who are interested in specific policy measures for looked after children are likely to find the discussion by Fitzpatrick (2009) helpful.

In addition to policy changes, each school needs to make certain curriculum adjustments to ensure that all the Articles relevant to schools are covered adequately in the range of subjects taught.

To help schools with their policy formulation, in addition to the template policy in Appendix C, the full text of the UNCRC is also provided in Appendix B. This will help schools to make informed decisions about their own Child Rights Policy, and associated curriculum.

## Know What Your Schoolchildren Really Think

Very few schools have a good grip on knowing what the children really think about the school, the teachers, and their learning.

Yes, many schools have something like a School Council when pupils can air their views, usually in a public situation.

What is missing in most schools is any mechanism to know what the children really think, and what concerns they really have.

The power distance between teachers and pupils acts as a very powerful inhibitor of children expressing many things they really think. Adults expect other adults to raise concerns and express them, hopefully without fear of any detriment. How many children feel free to tell a teacher that the lessons are boring, badly structured, or fail to provide real learning situations and motivation? - very few - they fear a variety of forms of retaliation and detriment.

Who really knows if there are problems with the school, or a particular teacher? - the children.

Of course teachers and schools would prefer they have no problems, and many would like to 'bury their heads in the sand' and not know about, or procrastinate in dealing with, problems that are obvious to the children.

This does not mean that by introducing a mechanism for children to express their concerns, the teachers will be drawn into some kind of popularity contest. That is a danger arising from some performance measurement exercises such as the UK's National Student Survey (NSS) measures of student 'satisfaction' applied to higher education institutions; some universities introduce NSS scores as part of the mechanism to appraise lecturer performance. That really can be a mechanism to subvert good lecturing and teaching because the lecturers can be measured on the subjective statements of students! I am certainly not advocating that for schools.

Many schools have mechanisms in place to manage suspicions of poor teaching practice. For example, a head of department may observe the lessons of a teacher. What often happens? - while being observed, the lessons are very good! The children know what has happened, but school management doesn't. I have seen many instances of that happening. The result is that it can take years for school management to deal with poor teachers.

A popularity contest is not necessary. I have seen many instances (and I am sure so have many readers) of teachers who are considered by the children to be very strict, but notwithstanding that, the teacher is appreciated by the children because the children know that real learning is taking place.

It is important to keep in mind that for most children in school, their first priority is to feel they are learning. A teacher does not need to be particularly nice, but a teacher does need to ensure that effective learning has taken place. If a teacher can produce effective learning, and be nice at the same time, there is an added bonus.

The bottom line is that the people who know best who are the effective teachers and who are the weak teachers, are the children.

Yes, if there is an opportunity for children to provide anonymous feedback and comments, there will be cases of malicious and ill-founded allegations. Mechanisms to manage child feedback need to be sensitive to this reality. However, one strong message that comes out of several of the child protection case reviews is the number of times children raised concerns but were not listened too.

The suggestion to enable children to provide anonymous feedback and comments about their school and learning is one of the most effective ways a school can know what is really going on in the school. Most schools simply have no idea what the children really think. In a very real sense, many schools do not want to know!

When putting in place a mechanism for children to say what they think, there are three important contexts to keep in mind:

1. anonymity
2. confidentiality

3. openness

Offering the possibility of raising concerns anonymously is one way the school can avoid fear of the power distance relationship between teachers and children inhibiting disclosure of concerns. Children need to be told that if concerns are expressed anonymously, there may be limitations on what can be done, particularly if the concerns are really about issues between specific people. However, a school should not prevent this kind of freedom of expression. The other key advice to children is to express their concerns genuinely and in good faith, and never use the opportunity to be malicious or spiteful.

If a concern is expressed without anonymity, the person expressing the concern will often need the initial assurance of confidentiality.

However, confidentiality is more tricky, especially in the UK because of its muddle over confidentiality and safeguarding with respect to sexual offences. If a disclosure is made about a situation involving a child and a child protection issue, adults may be required by law to break confidentiality - unless the situation involves a sexual offence, which in many cases will result in the preservation of confidentiality - the child cannot predict if confidentiality will be preserved or not. However, for concerns over learning or teacher conduct in the classroom, there should be no problem guaranteeing confidentiality.

Openness is the easiest for raising and dealing with issues, but the greatest fear of a child is suffering some form of detriment.

The bottom line for schools, is that unless they provide the children with an opportunity to express what they feel, and raise any concerns anonymously if they wish, and without detriment, the school is at best weak, or at worst deaf and blind to what is really going on. Encourage children to be frank and honest and put mechanisms in place to encourage children to make anonymous disclosures. Tap into the most effective resource to know what's going on.

[figure 5.1 on next page]

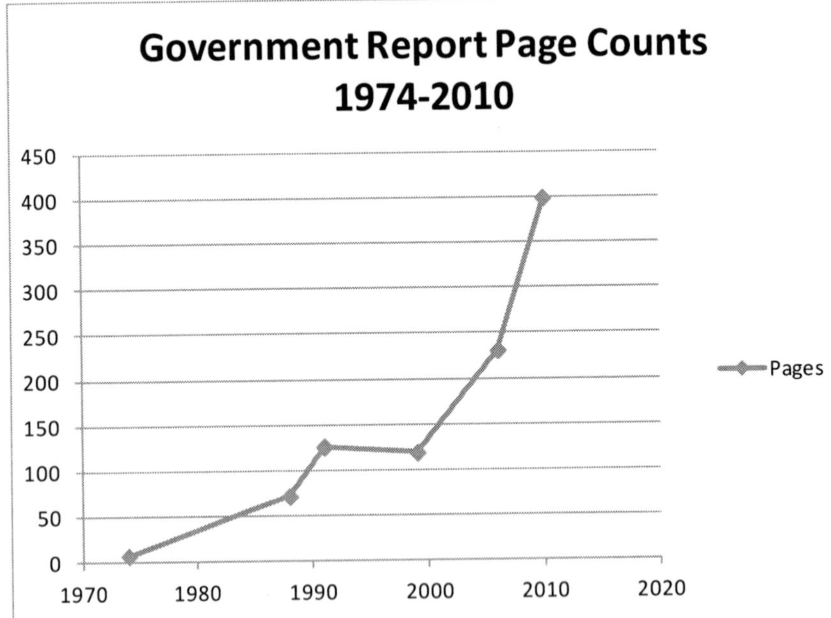


**Figure 5.1 Government Report Page Counts (after Parton, 2011).**

# Teacher Self-Evaluation

## Psychological Abuse Scale For Teachers

**Wayne Nesbit © - reproduced by permission[1]**

This set of questions has been reproduced by kind permission of the original author. It can be used by teachers as a self-evaluation checklist.

The questions are divided into subcategories of abuse (see the original publication for further information): demeaning; discriminating; dominating; destabilizing; distancing; and diverse.

Please note that this questionnaire is copyright. The copyright holder is Prof. Wayne Nesbit. You should not reproduce it without his permission. It is ok to make a copy for the purposes of the purchaser of the book completing it, or sending a copy to the book publisher should you wish, but it should not be copied further without permission.

The questionnaire is for purposes of self-evaluation. Go through the questions and attempt to answer each question as honestly as possible. That will give you a good indication of any classroom behaviour which you should consider adjusting. If you are feeling brave, you can involve others who know you, and ask for their help in deciding how you should answer.

1 "Psychological Abuse Scale for Teachers" in Nesbit, W.C. (1991) Mutilation of the Spirit: the Educational Context of Emotional Abuse. St. Johns: Memorial University of Newfoundland and Newfoundland Council for Exceptional Children. pp187-192.

**Demeaning**

| Q | Question | Never | Infrequently | Often | Very Often |
|---|---|---|---|---|---|
| 1 | Is my criticism destructive .... undermining students' best efforts? | | | | |
| 2 | Do I verbally belittle students using sarcasm and offensive labels (i.e., childish, lazy, motor-mouth)? | | | | |
| 3 | Do I make comparisons that humiliate or embarrass (use mistakes as class examples, return tests in rank order)? | | | | |
| 4 | Do I berate or reprimand students in front of others? | | | | |
| 5 | Do I, in a child's presence, discuss his problems with others ... as if he were not there? | | | | |
| 6 | Do I react in ways which embarrass students when they ask questions? | | | | |
| 7 | Do I focus and dwell upon a student's one bad habit? | | | | |
| 8 | Do my disciplinary methods (i.e., verbal put-downs) degrade students? | | | | |
| 9 | Is there sarcasm or mockery in my humor (i.e., obtaining a laugh at the student's expense)? | | | | |
| 10 | Do I snicker or joke about a student's poor performance or tolerate laughter and abuse from his peers? | | | | |
| 11 | Does my treatment of classroom discussion topics (i.e.. divorce, teenage pregnancy, poverty) make students uncomfortable? | | | | |
| 12 | Do students echo my negative sentiments about themselves? | | | | |

**Discriminating**

| Q | Question | Never | Infrequently | Often | Very Often |
|---|---|---|---|---|---|
| 13 | Do I make private or in-class comparisons between brighter children and those with learning difficulties? | | | | |
| 14 | Does a child's intellectual ability negatively influence how I interact with him? | | | | |
| 15 | Do I choose the "better" students to contribute when conducting an "open" class discussion? | | | | |
| 16 | Do I single out particular students for criticism, correction, or reprimand? | | | | |
| 17 | Do I discipline some children more severely than others for the *same* misbehavior? | | | | |
| 18 | Do I derive satisfaction from reprimanding particular students? | | | | |
| 19 | Do I discriminate against ethnically different children by ignoring their input or by general insensitivity to their background and values? | | | | |
| 20 | Are my lessons, instructional examples, or marking strategies offensive to particular ethnic/social groups? | | | | |
| 21 | Do I present sexist interpretations of curriculum content or make sexually biased comments? | | | | |
| 22 | Do I make predetermined judgements about a child's chance for success in life based upon sex, familial considerations, ethnic background, or economic level'? | | | | |

**Dominating**

| Q | Question | Never | Infrequently | Often | Very Often |
|---|---|---|---|---|---|
| 23 | Are my classes overly quiet? | | | | |
| 24 | Does my teaching consist of structured content and rote activities? | | | | |
| 25 | Do I raise my voice in frustration and anger? | | | | |
| 26 | Do I stare to discourage input and challenge? | | | | |
| 27 | Do I employ failure and threats of failure to maintain control? | | | | |
| 28 | When challenged, is my immediate reaction negative? | | | | |
| 29 | Do I interrupt student responses and insert my views before they have had time to formulate answers? | | | | |
| 30 | Do I use sarcasm and criticism to diminish a student's negative role model capability)? | | | | |
| 31 | Do I deny students a part in decision-making? | | | | |

**Destabilizing**

| Q | Question | Never | Infrequently | Often | Very Often |
|---|---|---|---|---|---|
| 32 | Is there an uncomfortable tension when I enter the classroom? | | | | |
| 33 | Do students "shy away" from asking or answering questions ... from seeking assistance? | | | | |
| 34 | Are students reluctant to admit when they don't understand? | | | | |
| 35 | Is there a lack of general spontaneity in my classroom? | | | | |
| 36 | Do I create worry and stress by expecting too much of students, irrespective of ability? | | | | |
| 37 | Do I insist that students answer questions even when I am aware that they do not know the correct responses? | | | | |
| 38 | Do I pressure "inhibited" students with regard to oral reading and participation | | | | |
| 39 | Are students intimidated and visibly upset when I approach or ask a question (i.e., lowering eyes, tensing muscles, trembling, stumbling over words)? | | | | |
| 40 | Do I physically threaten students (i.e.. banging pointer on desk, circling students' desks)? | | | | |
| 41 | Are students frequently absent from my classes? | | | | |

**Distancing**

| Q | Question | Never | Infrequently | Often | Very Often |
|---|---|---|---|---|---|
| 42 | Would my approach to students be different if they were my own children? | | | | |
| 43 | Is my involvement with students defined by school hours and restricted to large group discussions? | | | | |
| 44 | Do I "talk down" to students, downplaying or disregarding their ideas? | | | | |
| 45 | Does my vocal tone and/or body language (i.e., eye contact) convey a cold business-like detachment? | | | | |
| 46 | Do my classes lack humor and good natured give-and-take? | | | | |
| 47 | Do students perceive me as lacking empathy, sincerity and sensitivity? Too busy to be a friend or confidant? | | | | |
| 48 | Do students act differently toward me (i.e.. unresponsive, lacking warmth) than they do toward other teachers? | | | | |

## Diverse

| Q | Question | Never | Infrequently | Often | Very Often |
|---|---|---|---|---|---|
| 49 | Do I "fly off the handle" and regret things I have said to the class or an individual student? | | | | |
| 50 | Do I make accusations without knowing all the facts? | | | | |
| 51 | Am I impatient when slower students require more time to complete tasks? | | | | |
| 52 | Am I inconsistent? Do my moods negatively influence student treatment? | | | | |
| 53 | Do I allow personal life problems to effect the quality of my relationships with students? | | | | |
| 54 | If I were interacting with adults, would I treat them in a different fashion? | | | | |
| 55 | Would students and others describe my classroom behaviors as abusive? | | | | |

# Pupil Self-Evaluation

## Psychological Abuse Scale For Pupils

This version of the Questionnaire is the first version to start collecting pupil data about their experiences of emotional abuse in the classroom.

For each question, put a tick or cross in the relevant answer. Also, please indicate if the incidents that you have experienced have been in the past, or if they still happen sometimes.

If you would like to give examples of any incidents, or provide feedback for any of the questions, please use the form at the end of the questionnaire to do so. Please use continuation sheets if necessary.

Thank you for participating. All responses will be treated in the strictest confidence, and anonymity is assured.

Please note that this questionnaire is copyright Geoffrey Darnton. It should not be copied and circulated without permission. It may be copied by the purchaser of the book to have a copy to complete. It may be copied for completion to send to the author.

This Psychological Abuse Scale for Pupils has been derived from the Psychological Abuse Scale for Teachers in Nesbit, W.C. (1991) *Mutilation of the Spirit: the Educational Context of Emotional Abuse.* St. Johns: Memorial University of Newfoundland and Newfoundland Council for Exceptional Children. pp187-192. All derivations are entirely GD's responsibility and Nesbit's original work is acknowledged. The questions 'inverted' from the original teacher scale have been supplemented by further questions.

First, some basic information about you:

| **Age:** | **Sex:** M: F: | **School Year:** | **School Type:** |
|---|---|---|---|
| | | | |

**Questions Relating to Demeaning Conduct**

| Q | Question | Never | Infrequently | Often | Very Often | In the Past | Still happens sometimes |
|---|---|---|---|---|---|---|---|
| 1 | Do you think your best efforts have ever been undermined by destructive teacher criticism? | | | | | | |
| 2 | Have you ever been belittled by a teacher using sarcasm or labels you considered offensive (e.g. childish, lazy)? | | | | | | |
| 3 | Have you ever been humiliated or embarrassed by a teacher making comparisons that included you (using any of your mistakes as an example, or listing class results in rank order)? | | | | | | |
| 4 | Have you ever been 'put-down' or 'told off' in front of others? | | | | | | |
| 5 | Has a teacher ever discussed any of your problems with others in front of you, as though you were not there? | | | | | | |

| Q | Question | Never | Infrequently | Often | Very Often | In the Past | Still happens sometimes |
|---|---|---|---|---|---|---|---|
| 6 | Has a teacher ever embarrassed you by the way they react to your questions? | | | | | | |
| 7 | Has a teacher ever focussed and dwelt on what the teacher considered to be one of your bad habits? | | | | | | |
| 8 | Have any disciplinary methods used by a teacher ever made you feel degraded? | | | | | | |
| 9 | Has a teacher ever used sarcasm or mockery in their humour (i.e. obtaining a laugh from others at your expense)? | | | | | | |
| 10 | Has a teacher ever snickered or joked about your performance in school work? | | | | | | |
| 11 | Has a teacher ever tolerated laughter about or abuse to you, from your classmates? | | | | | | |
| 12 | Have you felt uncomfortable about some classroom discussion topics (about things like divorce, teenage pregnancy, poverty) because of the way the teacher has treated those topics? | | | | | | |
| 13 | Do you repeat or accept any negative teacher sentiments about you? | | | | | | |

## Questions Relating to Discriminating Conduct

| Q | Question | Never | Infrequently | Often | Very Often | In the Past | Still happens sometimes |
|---|---|---|---|---|---|---|---|
| 14 | Has a teacher ever made any private or in-class comparisons between you and others when you were experiencing any learning difficulties? | | | | | | |
| 15 | Has a teacher ever refused to accept you have difficulty understanding something when you really did have such difficulty? | | | | | | |
| 16 | Has a teacher ever refused to help you but helped another of your classmates? | | | | | | |
| 17 | Have you ever felt that a teacher has interacted with you negatively because of what you think is the teacher's view of your intellectual ability? | | | | | | |
| 18 | When there is an open class discussion, has a teacher ever chosen pupils other than you to contribute, and ignored your attempts to contribute? | | | | | | |
| 19 | Has a teacher ever singled you out for criticism, correction, or reprimand more than most others in your class? | | | | | | |
| 20 | Do you think your conduct in class has ever been worse than most of your classmates? | | | | | | |

| Q | Question | Never | Infrequently | Often | Very Often | In the Past | Still happens sometimes |
|---|---|---|---|---|---|---|---|
| 21 | Has a teacher ever disciplined you more severely than others for the *same* misbehaviour? | | | | | | |
| 22 | Do you think a teacher has ever derived satisfaction from reprimanding particular students? | | | | | | |
| 23 | Has a teacher ever discriminated against ethnically different children by ignoring their input or by general insensitivity to their background and values? | | | | | | |
| 24 | Have you ever experienced any lessons, instructional examples, or marking strategies you consider could be offensive to particular ethnic/social groups? | | | | | | |
| 25 | Has a teacher ever presented sexist interpretations of curriculum content or make sexually biased comments? | | | | | | |
| 26 | Has a teacher ever made predetermined judgements about your chance for success in life based upon sex, familial considerations, ethnic background, or economic level? | | | | | | |
| 27 | Has a teacher ever made predetermined judgements about you because of a brother or sister? | | | | | | |

| Q | Question | Never | Infrequently | Often | Very Often | In the Past | Still happens sometimes |
|---|---|---|---|---|---|---|---|
| 28 | Has a teacher ever made predetermined judgements about you because your friendship with another person? | | | | | | |

## Questions Relating to Dominating Conduct

| Q | Question | Never | Infrequently | Often | Very Often | In the Past | Still happens sometimes |
|---|---|---|---|---|---|---|---|
| 29 | Have you ever been in classes that have seemed too quiet to you? | | | | | | |
| 30 | Have you ever been taught by a teacher who has used only structured content and rote activities? | | | | | | |
| 31 | Has a teacher ever raised their voice to you in frustration and anger? | | | | | | |
| 32 | Has a teacher ever stared at you to discourage input and challenge? | | | | | | |
| 33 | Has a teacher ever used failure and threats of failure to try to maintain control over you? | | | | | | |
| 34 | Have you ever experienced a teacher whose immediate reaction is negative when challenged? | | | | | | |
| 35 | Has a teacher ever interrupted your responses to his/her question and inserted their views before you have had time to formulate answers? | | | | | | |

| Q | Question | Never | Infrequently | Often | Very Often | In the Past | Still happens sometimes |
|---|---|---|---|---|---|---|---|
| 36 | Have you ever experienced a teacher using sarcasm and criticism in an attempt to get you to see the teacher in a positive light? (i.e. stop you using the teacher as a negative role model)? | | | | | | |
| 37 | Has a teacher ever denied you a part in decision-making? | | | | | | |

## Questions Relating to Destabilizing Conduct

| Q | Question | Never | Infrequently | Often | Very Often | In the Past | Still happens sometimes |
|---|---|---|---|---|---|---|---|
| 38 | Has any teacher usually caused uncomfortable tension when they enter your classroom? | | | | | | |
| 39 | Have there been any teachers from whom you would "shy away" from asking or answering questions ... or from seeking assistance? | | | | | | |
| 40 | Have you ever felt reluctant to admit to a teacher you don't understand something? | | | | | | |
| 41 | Have you ever been in a class where there is a lack of general spontaneity? | | | | | | |
| 42 | Has a teacher ever created worry and stress in you by expecting too much of you, irrespective of your ability? | | | | | | |
| 43 | Has a teacher ever insisted that you answer questions even when the teacher is likely to be aware that you do not know the correct responses? | | | | | | |
| 44 | Have you ever been pressured by a teacher with regard to oral reading and participation even if you felt "inhibited"? | | | | | | |

| Q | Question | Never | Infrequently | Often | Very Often | In the Past | Still happens sometimes |
|---|---|---|---|---|---|---|---|
| 45 | Have you ever been intimidated and visibly upset (visible in ways such as lowering your eyes, tensing your muscles, trembling, stumbling over words) when a teacher approached you or asked you a question? | | | | | | |
| 46 | Have you ever felt physically threatened by a teacher (in ways such as the teacher banging a pointer on desk, circling your desk, standing too close to you)? | | | | | | |
| 47 | Have you ever been hit or touched by a teacher during a disagreement with the teacher? | | | | | | |
| 48 | Have you ever been absent from a teacher's classes because of how you felt about the teacher? | | | | | | |

## Questions Relating to Distancing Conduct

| Q | Question | Never | Infrequently | Often | Very Often | In the Past | Still happens sometimes |
|---|---|---|---|---|---|---|---|
| 49 | Do you think a teacher has ever approached you differently than if you were the teacher's own child? | | | | | | |
| 50 | Have you ever experienced a teacher whose involvement with you is defined by school hours? | | | | | | |
| 51 | Have you ever experienced a teacher whose involvement with you is restricted to large group discussions? | | | | | | |
| 52 | Have you ever been "talked down" to by a teacher down playing or disregarding your ideas? | | | | | | |
| 53 | Has a teacher ever conveyed to you a cold business-like detachment by their vocal tone and/or body language (i.e., eye contact)? | | | | | | |
| 54 | Have you ever had classes that lack humour and good natured give-and-take? | | | | | | |
| 55 | Have you ever been able to interact with a teacher as a friend or confidant? | | | | | | |

| Q | Question | Never | Infrequently | Often | Very Often | In the Past | Still happens sometimes |
|---|---|---|---|---|---|---|---|
| 56 | Are there any teachers you have ever perceived as lacking empathy, sincerity and sensitivity so the teacher could not be a friend or confidant? | | | | | | |
| 57 | Have there ever been teachers you act differently towards because of certain characteristics (i.e., unresponsive, lacking warmth) than you do toward other teachers? | | | | | | |

## Diverse Questions

| Q | Question | Never | Infrequently | Often | Very Often | In the Past | Still happens sometimes |
|---|---|---|---|---|---|---|---|
| 58 | Has a teacher ever expressed regret about saying things to the class or you after "flying off the handle"? | | | | | | |
| 59 | Have you ever been accused of something by a teacher who did not know all the facts? | | | | | | |
| 60 | Have you ever been accused of something by a teacher you knew to be wrong? | | | | | | |
| 61 | Has a teacher ever been impatient with you because you really require more time to complete tasks? | | | | | | |
| 62 | Has a teacher ever treated you negatively or inconsistently because of the teacher's moods? | | | | | | |
| 63 | Has your relationship with a teacher ever been affected by the personal life problems of the teacher? | | | | | | |
| 64 | Has a teacher ever interacted with you in a way that is very different from the way you think the teacher would interact with adults? | | | | | | |
| 65 | Have you experienced any teachers for whom you would describe their classroom behaviour as abusive? | | | | | | |

**Additional comments or example(s):**

| Relating to Question No: | Comment(s) or Example(s) |
|---|---|
| | |
| | |
| | |
| | |
| | |
| | |
| | |
| | |
| | |
| | |

# The Good, the Bad, and the Ugly...

To coin the title of the famous movie, the goal of this Chapter is to present information about good, bad, and ugly stories, experiences and memories of the classroom and school situation.

Earlier chapters presented self-evaluation questionnaires for both teachers and pupils. These can be copied and sent in if you wish to submit your responses. They will all be treated confidentially, and do not need any identifying information. You are encouraged to submit via the website, http://ClassroomEmotionalAbuse.com/, where you can also obtain up-to-date information about how to send any stories, experiences, memories, or comments.

Although the primary focus of this book is emotional abuse in the classroom, please send in stories about things that happened to you to make you feel very happy about school, or which have left you with long-term positive memories of school. It will be of enormous assistance to teachers to understand what to do in the classroom, and what to avoid doing.

## The Good ...

Experiences, stories, and memories of what made pupils feel particularly good in terms of classroom experiences.

This is intended to present information about what made pupils feel good. It is not a judgmental, objective summary; it is subjective, based on how pupils, or ex-pupils *feel* about their experiences and memories.

Examples could include:

- lessons you feel really helped your learning
- ways in which a teacher handled an academic or personal situation, and left you feeling really good
- a teacher who has had a positive influence on you for many years, or who you are always happy reflecting on your classes with the teacher
- any experience or memory of a teacher handling a situation particularly well

- experiences or memories of what a teacher did to earn your respect
- ... any other experiences or memories leaving you feeling 'good'

## The Bad ...

Experiences, stories, and memories of what made pupils feel particularly bad in terms of classroom experiences.

As with things that made pupils feel 'good', this is intended to present information about what made pupils feel bad. It is not a judgmental, objective summary; it is subjective, based on how pupils, or ex-pupils *feel* about their experiences and memories.

Emphasis here is on situations that made pupils feel bad; it is not for 'normal' situations which were neither memorably good nor memorably bad- i.e. not-exceptional.

Examples could include:

- lessons where the teacher's approach resulted in a feeling of little or no learning
- classes where any of the items identified in the pupil self-evaluation questionnaire were repeated multiple times
- classes or teachers that you tried to avoid for some reason
- teachers who were very arbitrary in what they expected
- teachers who were generally intimidating without corresponding effective learning
- ...any other experiences or memories leaving you feeling 'bad'

## The Ugly ...

The 'ugly' is for experiences, stories, and memories of things that should not have happened. A teacher doing something 'ugly' is probably taking a risk of being fired from the teaching job, or some other agency having serious concerns if it knew what had happened.

Examples could include:

- blackmail of any kind
- aggressive behaviour - physical or psychological
- destruction of a child's self-esteem
- encouraging, condoning, participating in, or failing to act on any unlawful activity
- ...any other experiences or memories of unacceptable behaviour

# Definitions

**corporal punishment**
any disciplinary procedure involving the body

**corporal punishment with physical pain**
any disciplinary procedure intended to inflict physical pain, or which actually causes physical pain

**corporal punishment without physical pain**
any disciplinary procedure that is not intended to inflict physical pain, does not actually inflict physical pain, and involves the body

**emotional abuse**
the use of words or expressions directed at other people, reckless or intentional as to the possibility of maltreatment, injury or hurt to those others

**preventative disciplinary procedure**
any disciplinary procedure that is not punishment but is intended to prevent the occurrence or re-occurrence of misbehaviour

**punishment**
a procedure that decreases the chance that a misbehaviour will recur
[punishment has 3 classes:
1. corporal punishment - with physical pain
2. corporal punishment - without physical pain
3. non-corporal punishment]

**retaliation**
any procedure following an event inflicted because of the event - the procedure may involve inflicting pain or not, or, some undesired inconvenience

**retribution**

any procedure that is punishment or retaliation, and which involves the misbehaver doing something for the benefit of the victim of the misbehaviour.

# International Declarations of the Rights of the Child

## Geneva Declaration of the Rights of the Child

Adopted 26 September, 1924, League of Nations

### Geneva Declaration of the Rights of the Child

By the present Declaration of the Rights of the Child, commonly known as "Declaration of Geneva," men and women of all nations, recognizing that mankind owes to the Child the best that it has to give, declare and accept it as their duty that, beyond and above all considerations of race, nationality or creed:

1. The child must be given the means requisite for its normal development, both materially and spiritually;

2. The child that is hungry must be fed; the child that is sick must be nursed; the child that is backward must be helped; the delinquent child must be reclaimed; and the orphan and the waif must be sheltered and succoured;

3. The child must be the first to receive relief in times of distress;

4. The child must be put in a position to earn a livelihood, and must be protected against every form of exploitation;

5. The child must be brought up in the consciousness that its talents must be devoted to the service of fellow men.

(from League of Nations, 1924)

## Declaration of the Rights of the Child[1]

Adopted by UN General Assembly Resolution 1386 (XIV) of 10 December 1959

WHEREAS the peoples of the United Nations have, in the Charter, reaffirmed their faith in fundamental human rights and in the dignity and worth of the human person, and have determined to promote social progress and better standards of life in larger freedom,

WHEREAS the United Nations has, in the Universal Declaration of Human Rights, proclaimed that everyone is entitled to all the rights and freedoms set forth therein, without distinction of any kind, such as race, colour, sex, language, religion, political or other opinion, national or social origin, property, birth or other status,

WHEREAS the child, by reason of his physical and mental immaturity, needs special safeguards and care, including appropriate legal protection, before as well as after birth,

WHEREAS the need for such special safeguards has been stated in the Geneva Declaration of the Rights of the Child of 1924, and recognized in the Universal Declaration of Human Rights and in the statutes of specialized agencies and international organizations concerned with the welfare of children,

WHEREAS mankind owes to the child the best it has to give,

Now, therefore, *The General Assembly* Proclaims

THIS DECLARATION OF THE RIGHTS OF THE CHILD to the end that he may have a happy childhood and enjoy for his own good and for the good of society the rights and freedoms herein set forth, and calls upon parents, upon men and women as individuals, and upon voluntary organizations, local authorities and national Governments to recognize these rights and strive for their observance by legislative and other measures progressively taken in accordance with the following principles:

1. The child shall enjoy all the rights set forth in this Declaration. Every child, without any exception whatsoever, shall be entitled

1 UN (1978).

to these rights, without distinction or discrimination on account of race, colour, sex, language, religion, political or other opinion, national or social origin, property, birth or other status, whether of himself or of his family.

2. The child shall enjoy special protection, and shall be given opportunities and facilities, by law and by other means, to enable him to develop physically, mentally, morally, spiritually and socially in a healthy and normal manner and in conditions of freedom and dignity. In the enactment of laws for this purpose, the best interests of the child shall be the paramount consideration.

3. The child shall be entitled from his birth to a name and a nationality.

4. The child shall enjoy the benefits of social security. He shall be entitled to grow and develop in health; to this end, special care and protection shall be provided both to him and to his mother, including adequate pre-natal and post-natal care. The child shall have the right to adequate nutrition, housing, recreation and medical services.

5. The child who is physically, mentally or socially handicapped shall be given the special treatment, education and care required by his particular condition.

6. The child, for the full and harmonious development of his personality, needs love and understanding. He shall, wherever possible, grow up in the care and under the responsibility of his parents, and, in any case, in an atmosphere of affection and of moral and material security; a child of tender years shall not, save in exceptional circumstances, be separated from his mother. Society and the public authorities shall have the duty to extend particular care to children without a family and to those without adequate means of support. Payment of State and other assistance towards the maintenance of children of large families is desirable.

7. The child is entitled to receive education, which shall be free and compulsory, at least in the elementary stages. He shall be given an education which will promote his general culture and enable him, on a basis of equal opportunity, to develop his abilities, his individual judgement, and his sense of moral and social responsibility, and to become a useful member of society.

   The best interests of the child shall be the guiding principle of those responsible for his education and guidance; that responsibility lies in the first place with his parents.

   The child shall have full opportunity for play and recreation, which should be directed to the same purposes as education; society and the public authorities shall endeavour to promote the enjoyment of this right.

8. The child shall in all circumstances be among the first to receive protection and relief.

9. The child shall be protected against all forms of neglect, cruelty and exploitation. He shall not be the subject of traffic, in any form.

   The child shall not be admitted to employment before an appropriate minimum age; he shall in no case be caused or permitted to engage in any occupation or employment which would prejudice his health or education, or interfere with his physical, mental or moral development.

10. The child shall be protected from practices which may foster racial, religious and any other form of discrimination. He shall be brought up in a spirit of understanding, tolerance, friendship among peoples, peace and universal brotherhood, and in full consciousness that his energy and talents should be devoted to the service of his fellow men.

## UNDRC Plain Language Version

1. All children have the right to what follows, no matter what their race, colour sex, language, religion, political or other opinion, or where they were born or who they were born to.

2. You have the special right to grow up and to develop physically and spiritually in a healthy and normal way, free and with dignity.

3. You have a right to a name and to be a member of a country.

4. You have a right to special care and protection and to good food, housing and medical services.

5. You have the right to special care if handicapped in any way.

6. You have the right to love and understanding, preferably from parents and family, but from the government where these cannot help.

7. You have the right to go to school for free, to play, and to have an equal chance to develop yourself and to learn to be responsible and useful.

   Your parents have special responsibilities for your education and guidance.

8. You have the right always to be among the first to get help.

9. You have the right to be protected against cruel acts or exploitation, e.g. you shall not be obliged to do work which hinders your development both physically and mentally.

   You should not work before a minimum age and never when that would hinder your health, and your moral and physical development.

10. You should be taught peace, understanding, tolerance and friendship among all people.

(from UN, 1978)

## Convention on the Rights of the Child[2]

Adopted and opened for signature, ratification and accession by General Assembly resolution 44/25 of 20 November 1989

entry into force 2 September 1990, in accordance with article 49

### Preamble

The States Parties to the present Convention,

Considering that, in accordance with the principles proclaimed in the Charter of the United Nations, recognition of the inherent dignity and of the equal and inalienable rights of all members of the human family is the foundation of freedom, justice and peace in the world,

Bearing in mind that the peoples of the United Nations have, in the Charter, reaffirmed their faith in fundamental human rights and in the dignity and worth of the human person, and have determined to promote social progress and better standards of life in larger freedom,

Recognizing that the United Nations has, in the Universal Declaration of Human Rights and in the International Covenants on Human Rights, proclaimed and agreed that everyone is entitled to all the rights and freedoms set forth therein, without distinction of any kind, such as race, colour, sex, language, religion, political or other opinion, national or social origin, property, birth or other status,

Recalling that, in the Universal Declaration of Human Rights, the United Nations has proclaimed that childhood is entitled to special care and assistance,

Convinced that the family, as the fundamental group of society and the natural environment for the growth and well-being of all its members and particularly children, should be afforded the necessary protection and assistance so that it can fully assume its responsibilities within the community,

2 UNGA (1989)

Recognizing that the child, for the full and harmonious development of his or her personality, should grow up in a family environment, in an atmosphere of happiness, love and understanding,

Considering that the child should be fully prepared to live an individual life in society, and brought up in the spirit of the ideals proclaimed in the Charter of the United Nations, and in particular in the spirit of peace, dignity, tolerance, freedom, equality and solidarity,

Bearing in mind that the need to extend particular care to the child has been stated in the Geneva Declaration of the Rights of the Child of 1924 and in the Declaration of the Rights of the Child adopted by the General Assembly on 20 November 1959 and recognized in the Universal Declaration of Human Rights, in the International Covenant on Civil and Political Rights (in particular in articles 23 and 24), in the International Covenant on Economic, Social and Cultural Rights (in particular in article 10) and in the statutes and relevant instruments of specialized agencies and international organizations concerned with the welfare of children,

Bearing in mind that, as indicated in the Declaration of the Rights of the Child, "the child, by reason of his physical and mental immaturity, needs special safeguards and care, including appropriate legal protection, before as well as after birth",

Recalling the provisions of the Declaration on Social and Legal Principles relating to the Protection and Welfare of Children, with Special Reference to Foster Placement and Adoption Nationally and Internationally; the United Nations Standard Minimum Rules for the Administration of Juvenile Justice (The Beijing Rules) ; and the Declaration on the Protection of Women and Children in Emergency and Armed Conflict, Recognizing that, in all countries in the world, there are children living in exceptionally difficult conditions, and that such children need special consideration,

Taking due account of the importance of the traditions and cultural values of each people for the protection and harmonious development of the child, Recognizing the importance of international cooperation for improving the living conditions of children in every country, in particular in the developing countries,

Have agreed as follows:

# PART I

## Article 1

For the purposes of the present Convention, a child means every human being below the age of eighteen years unless under the law applicable to the child, majority is attained earlier.

## Article 2

1. States Parties shall respect and ensure the rights set forth in the present Convention to each child within their jurisdiction without discrimination of any kind, irrespective of the child's or his or her parent's or legal guardian's race, colour, sex, language, religion, political or other opinion, national, ethnic or social origin, property, disability, birth or other status.

2. States Parties shall take all appropriate measures to ensure that the child is protected against all forms of discrimination or punishment on the basis of the status, activities, expressed opinions, or beliefs of the child's parents, legal guardians, or family members.

## Article 3

1. In all actions concerning children, whether undertaken by public or private social welfare institutions, courts of law, administrative authorities or legislative bodies, the best interests of the child shall be a primary consideration.

2. States Parties undertake to ensure the child such protection and care as is necessary for his or her well-being, taking into account the rights and duties of his or her parents, legal guardians, or other individuals legally responsible for him or her, and, to this end, shall take all appropriate legislative and administrative measures.

3. States Parties shall ensure that the institutions, services and facilities responsible for the care or protection of children shall conform with the standards established by competent authorities, particularly in

the areas of safety, health, in the number and suitability of their staff, as well as competent supervision.

**Article 4**

States Parties shall undertake all appropriate legislative, administrative, and other measures for the implementation of the rights recognized in the present Convention. With regard to economic, social and cultural rights, States Parties shall undertake such measures to the maximum extent of their available resources and, where needed, within the framework of international co-operation.

**Article 5**

States Parties shall respect the responsibilities, rights and duties of parents or, where applicable, the members of the extended family or community as provided for by local custom, legal guardians or other persons legally responsible for the child, to provide, in a manner consistent with the evolving capacities of the child, appropriate direction and guidance in the exercise by the child of the rights recognized in the present Convention.

**Article 6**

1. States Parties recognize that every child has the inherent right to life.

2. States Parties shall ensure to the maximum extent possible the survival and development of the child.

**Article 7**

1. The child shall be registered immediately after birth and shall have the right from birth to a name, the right to acquire a nationality and as far as possible, the right to know and be cared for by his or her parents.

2. States Parties shall ensure the implementation of these rights in accordance with their national law and their obligations under the

relevant international instruments in this field, in particular where the child would otherwise be stateless.

## Article 8

1. States Parties undertake to respect the right of the child to preserve his or her identity, including nationality, name and family relations as recognized by law without unlawful interference.

2. Where a child is illegally deprived of some or all of the elements of his or her identity, States Parties shall provide appropriate assistance and protection, with a view to re-establishing speedily his or her identity.

## Article 9

1. States Parties shall ensure that a child shall not be separated from his or her parents against their will, except when competent authorities subject to judicial review determine, in accordance with applicable law and procedures, that such separation is necessary for the best interests of the child. Such determination may be necessary in a particular case such as one involving abuse or neglect of the child by the parents, or one where the parents are living separately and a decision must be made as to the child's place of residence.

2. In any proceedings pursuant to paragraph 1 of the present article, all interested parties shall be given an opportunity to participate in the proceedings and make their views known.

3. States Parties shall respect the right of the child who is separated from one or both parents to maintain personal relations and direct contact with both parents on a regular basis, except if it is contrary to the child's best interests.

4. Where such separation results from any action initiated by a State Party, such as the detention, imprisonment, exile, deportation or death (including death arising from any cause while the person is in the custody of the State) of one or both parents or of the child, that State Party shall, upon request, provide the parents, the child

or, if appropriate, another member of the family with the essential information concerning the whereabouts of the absent member(s) of the family unless the provision of the information would be detrimental to the well-being of the child. States Parties shall further ensure that the submission of such a request shall of itself entail no adverse consequences for the person(s) concerned.

### Article 10

1. In accordance with the obligation of States Parties under article 9, paragraph 1, applications by a child or his or her parents to enter or leave a State Party for the purpose of family reunification shall be dealt with by States Parties in a positive, humane and expeditious manner. States Parties shall further ensure that the submission of such a request shall entail no adverse consequences for the applicants and for the members of their family.

2. A child whose parents reside in different States shall have the right to maintain on a regular basis, save in exceptional circumstances personal relations and direct contacts with both parents. Towards that end and in accordance with the obligation of States Parties under article 9, paragraph 1, States Parties shall respect the right of the child and his or her parents to leave any country, including their own, and to enter their own country. The right to leave any country shall be subject only to such restrictions as are prescribed by law and which are necessary to protect the national security, public order (ordre public), public health or morals or the rights and freedoms of others and are consistent with the other rights recognized in the present Convention.

### Article 11

1. States Parties shall take measures to combat the illicit transfer and non-return of children abroad.

2. To this end, States Parties shall promote the conclusion of bilateral or multilateral agreements or accession to existing agreements.

## Article 12

1. States Parties shall assure to the child who is capable of forming his or her own views the right to express those views freely in all matters affecting the child, the views of the child being given due weight in accordance with the age and maturity of the child.

2. For this purpose, the child shall in particular be provided the opportunity to be heard in any judicial and administrative proceedings affecting the child, either directly, or through a representative or an appropriate body, in a manner consistent with the procedural rules of national law.

## Article 13

1. The child shall have the right to freedom of expression; this right shall include freedom to seek, receive and impart information and ideas of all kinds, regardless of frontiers, either orally, in writing or in print, in the form of art, or through any other media of the child's choice.

2. The exercise of this right may be subject to certain restrictions, but these shall only be such as are provided by law and are necessary:

(a) For respect of the rights or reputations of others; or

(b) For the protection of national security or of public order (ordre public), or of public health or morals.

## Article 14

1. States Parties shall respect the right of the child to freedom of thought, conscience and religion.

2. States Parties shall respect the rights and duties of the parents and, when applicable, legal guardians, to provide direction to the child in the exercise of his or her right in a manner consistent with the evolving capacities of the child.

3. Freedom to manifest one's religion or beliefs may be subject only to such limitations as are prescribed by law and are necessary to protect public safety, order, health or morals, or the fundamental rights and freedoms of others.

**Article 15**

1. States Parties recognize the rights of the child to freedom of association and to freedom of peaceful assembly.

2. No restrictions may be placed on the exercise of these rights other than those imposed in conformity with the law and which are necessary in a democratic society in the interests of national security or public safety, public order (ordre public), the protection of public health or morals or the protection of the rights and freedoms of others.

**Article 16**

1. No child shall be subjected to arbitrary or unlawful interference with his or her privacy, family, home or correspondence, nor to unlawful attacks on his or her honour and reputation.

2. The child has the right to the protection of the law against such interference or attacks.

**Article 17**

States Parties recognize the important function performed by the mass media and shall ensure that the child has access to information and material from a diversity of national and international sources, especially those aimed at the promotion of his or her social, spiritual and moral well-being and physical and mental health.

To this end, States Parties shall:

(a) Encourage the mass media to disseminate information and material of social and cultural benefit to the child and in accordance with the spirit of article 29;

(b) Encourage international co-operation in the production, exchange and dissemination of such information and material from a diversity of cultural, national and international sources;

(c) Encourage the production and dissemination of children's books;

(d) Encourage the mass media to have particular regard to the linguistic needs of the child who belongs to a minority group or who is indigenous;

(e) Encourage the development of appropriate guidelines for the protection of the child from information and material injurious to his or her well-being, bearing in mind the provisions of articles 13 and 18.

**Article 18**

1. States Parties shall use their best efforts to ensure recognition of the principle that both parents have common responsibilities for the upbringing and development of the child. Parents or, as the case may be, legal guardians, have the primary responsibility for the upbringing and development of the child. The best interests of the child will be their basic concern.

2. For the purpose of guaranteeing and promoting the rights set forth in the present Convention,
States Parties shall render appropriate assistance to parents and legal guardians in the performance of their child-rearing responsibilities and shall ensure the development of institutions, facilities and services for the care of children.

3. States Parties shall take all appropriate measures to ensure that children of working parents have the right to benefit from child-care services and facilities for which they are eligible.

**Article 19**

1. States Parties shall take all appropriate legislative, administrative, social and educational measures to protect the child from all forms

of physical or mental violence, injury or abuse, neglect or negligent treatment, maltreatment or exploitation, including sexual abuse, while in the care of parent(s), legal guardian(s) or any other person who has the care of the child.

2. Such protective measures should, as appropriate, include effective procedures for the establishment of social programmes to provide necessary support for the child and for those who have the care of the child, as well as for other forms of prevention and for identification, reporting, referral, investigation, treatment and follow-up of instances of child maltreatment described heretofore, and, as appropriate, for judicial involvement.

**Article 20**

1. A child temporarily or permanently deprived of his or her family environment, or in whose own best interests cannot be allowed to remain in that environment, shall be entitled to special protection and assistance provided by the State.

2. States Parties shall in accordance with their national laws ensure alternative care for such a child.

3. Such care could include, inter alia, foster placement, kafalah of Islamic law, adoption or if necessary placement in suitable institutions for the care of children. When considering solutions, due regard shall be paid to the desirability of continuity in a child's upbringing and to the child's ethnic, religious, cultural and linguistic background.

**Article 21**

States Parties that recognize and/or permit the system of adoption shall ensure that the best interests of the child shall be the paramount consideration and they shall:

(a) Ensure that the adoption of a child is authorized only by competent authorities who determine, in accordance with applicable law and procedures and on the basis of all pertinent and reliable information, that the adoption is permissible in view of the child's status concerning parents, relatives and legal guardians and that, if required, the persons concerned have given their informed consent to the adoption on the basis of such counselling as may be necessary;

(b) Recognize that inter-country adoption may be considered as an alternative means of child's care, if the child cannot be placed in a foster or an adoptive family or cannot in any suitable manner be cared for in the child's country of origin;

(c) Ensure that the child concerned by inter-country adoption enjoys safeguards and standards equivalent to those existing in the case of national adoption;

(d) Take all appropriate measures to ensure that, in inter-country adoption, the placement does not result in improper financial gain for those involved in it;

(e) Promote, where appropriate, the objectives of the present article by concluding bilateral or multilateral arrangements or agreements, and endeavour, within this framework, to ensure that the placement of the child in another country is carried out by competent authorities or organs.

## Article 22

1. States Parties shall take appropriate measures to ensure that a child who is seeking refugee status or who is considered a refugee in accordance with applicable international or domestic law and procedures shall, whether unaccompanied or accompanied by his or her parents or by any other person, receive appropriate protection and humanitarian assistance in the enjoyment of applicable rights set forth in the present Convention and in other international human rights or humanitarian instruments to which the said States are Parties.

2. For this purpose, States Parties shall provide, as they consider appropriate, co-operation in any efforts by the United Nations and other competent intergovernmental organizations or non-governmental organizations co-operating with the United Nations

to protect and assist such a child and to trace the parents or other members of the family of any refugee child in order to obtain information necessary for reunification with his or her family. In cases where no parents or other members of the family can be found, the child shall be accorded the same protection as any other child permanently or temporarily deprived of his or her family environment for any reason , as set forth in the present Convention.

**Article 23**

1. States Parties recognize that a mentally or physically disabled child should enjoy a full and decent life, in conditions which ensure dignity, promote self-reliance and facilitate the child's active participation in the community.

2. States Parties recognize the right of the disabled child to special care and shall encourage and ensure the extension, subject to available resources, to the eligible child and those responsible for his or her care, of assistance for which application is made and which is appropriate to the child's condition and to the circumstances of the parents or others caring for the child.

3. Recognizing the special needs of a disabled child, assistance extended in accordance with paragraph 2 of the present article shall be provided free of charge, whenever possible, taking into account the financial resources of the parents or others caring for the child, and shall be designed to ensure that the disabled child has effective access to and receives education, training, health care services, rehabilitation services, preparation for employment and recreation opportunities in a manner conducive to the child's achieving the fullest possible social integration and individual development, including his or her cultural and spiritual development

4. States Parties shall promote, in the spirit of international cooperation, the exchange of appropriate information in the field of preventive health care and of medical, psychological and functional treatment of disabled children, including dissemination of and access to information concerning methods of rehabilitation, education and vocational services, with the aim of enabling States Parties to

improve their capabilities and skills and to widen their experience in these areas. In this regard, particular account shall be taken of the needs of developing countries.

**Article 24**

1. States Parties recognize the right of the child to the enjoyment of the highest attainable standard of health and to facilities for the treatment of illness and rehabilitation of health. States Parties shall strive to ensure that no child is deprived of his or her right of access to such health care services.

2. States Parties shall pursue full implementation of this right and, in particular, shall take appropriate measures:

(a) To diminish infant and child mortality;

(b) To ensure the provision of necessary medical assistance and health care to all children with emphasis on the development of primary health care;

(c) To combat disease and malnutrition, including within the framework of primary health care, through, inter alia, the application of readily available technology and through the provision of adequate nutritious foods and clean drinking-water, taking into consideration the dangers and risks of environmental pollution;

(d) To ensure appropriate pre-natal and post-natal health care for mothers;

(e) To ensure that all segments of society, in particular parents and children, are informed, have access to education and are supported in the use of basic knowledge of child health and nutrition, the advantages of breast-feeding, hygiene and environmental sanitation and the prevention of accidents;

(f) To develop preventive health care, guidance for parents and family planning education and services.

3. States Parties shall take all effective and appropriate measures with a view to abolishing traditional practices prejudicial to the health of children.

4. States Parties undertake to promote and encourage international co-operation with a view to achieving progressively the full realization of the right recognized in the present article. In this regard, particular account shall be taken of the needs of developing countries.

**Article 25**

States Parties recognize the right of a child who has been placed by the competent authorities for the purposes of care, protection or treatment of his or her physical or mental health, to a periodic review of the treatment provided to the child and all other circumstances relevant to his or her placement.

**Article 26**

1. States Parties shall recognize for every child the right to benefit from social security, including social insurance, and shall take the necessary measures to achieve the full realization of this right in accordance with their national law.

2. The benefits should, where appropriate, be granted, taking into account the resources and the circumstances of the child and persons having responsibility for the maintenance of the child, as well as any other consideration relevant to an application for benefits made by or on behalf of the child.

**Article 27**

1. States Parties recognize the right of every child to a standard of living adequate for the child's physical, mental, spiritual, moral and social development.

2. The parent(s) or others responsible for the child have the primary responsibility to secure, within their abilities and financial capacities, the conditions of living necessary for the child's development.

3. States Parties, in accordance with national conditions and within their means, shall take appropriate measures to assist parents and others responsible for the child to implement this right and shall in case of need provide material assistance and support programmes, particularly with regard to nutrition, clothing and housing.

4. States Parties shall take all appropriate measures to secure the recovery of maintenance for the child from the parents or other persons having financial responsibility for the child, both within the State Party and from abroad. In particular, where the person having financial responsibility for the child lives in a State different from that of the child, States Parties shall promote the accession to international agreements or the conclusion of such agreements, as well as the making of other appropriate arrangements.

## Article 28

1. States Parties recognize the right of the child to education, and with a view to achieving this right progressively and on the basis of equal opportunity, they shall, in particular:

(a) Make primary education compulsory and available free to all;

(b) Encourage the development of different forms of secondary education, including general and vocational education, make them available and accessible to every child, and take appropriate measures such as the introduction of free education and offering financial assistance in case of need;

(c) Make higher education accessible to all on the basis of capacity by every appropriate means;

(d) Make educational and vocational information and guidance available and accessible to all children; (e) Take measures to encourage regular attendance at schools and the reduction of drop-out rates.

2. States Parties shall take all appropriate measures to ensure that school discipline is administered in a manner consistent with the child's human dignity and in conformity with the present Convention.

3. States Parties shall promote and encourage international cooperation in matters relating to education, in particular with a view to contributing to the elimination of ignorance and illiteracy throughout the world and facilitating access to scientific and technical knowledge and modern teaching methods. In this regard, particular account shall be taken of the needs of developing countries.

**Article 29**

1. States Parties agree that the education of the child shall be directed to:

(a) The development of the child's personality, talents and mental and physical abilities to their fullest potential;

(b) The development of respect for human rights and fundamental freedoms, and for the principles enshrined in the Charter of the United Nations;

(c) The development of respect for the child's parents, his or her own cultural identity, language and values, for the national values of the country in which the child is living, the country from which he or she may originate, and for civilizations different from his or her own;

(d) The preparation of the child for responsible life in a free society, in the spirit of understanding, peace, tolerance, equality of sexes, and friendship among all peoples, ethnic, national and religious groups and persons of indigenous origin;

(e) The development of respect for the natural environment.

2. No part of the present article or article 28 shall be construed so as to interfere with the liberty of individuals and bodies to establish and direct educational institutions, subject always to the observance of the principle set forth in paragraph 1 of the present article and to the requirements that the education given in such institutions shall conform to such minimum standards as may be laid down by the State.

## Article 30

In those States in which ethnic, religious or linguistic minorities or persons of indigenous origin exist, a child belonging to such a minority or who is indigenous shall not be denied the right, in community with other members of his or her group, to enjoy his or her own culture, to profess and practise his or her own religion, or to use his or her own language.

## Article 31

1. States Parties recognize the right of the child to rest and leisure, to engage in play and recreational activities appropriate to the age of the child and to participate freely in cultural life and the arts.

2. States Parties shall respect and promote the right of the child to participate fully in cultural and artistic life and shall encourage the provision of appropriate and equal opportunities for cultural, artistic, recreational and leisure activity.

## Article 32

1. States Parties recognize the right of the child to be protected from economic exploitation and from performing any work that is likely to be hazardous or to interfere with the child's education, or to be harmful to the child's health or physical, mental, spiritual, moral or social development.

2. States Parties shall take legislative, administrative, social and educational measures to ensure the implementation of the present article. To this end, and having regard to the relevant provisions of other international instruments, States Parties shall in particular:

(a) Provide for a minimum age or minimum ages for admission to employment;

(b) Provide for appropriate regulation of the hours and conditions of employment;

(c) Provide for appropriate penalties or other sanctions to ensure the effective enforcement of the present article.

**Article 33**

States Parties shall take all appropriate measures, including legislative, administrative, social and educational measures, to protect children from the illicit use of narcotic drugs and psychotropic substances as defined in the relevant international treaties, and to prevent the use of children in the illicit production and trafficking of such substances.

**Article 34**

States Parties undertake to protect the child from all forms of sexual exploitation and sexual abuse. For these purposes, States Parties shall in particular take all appropriate national, bilateral and multilateral measures to prevent:

(a) The inducement or coercion of a child to engage in any unlawful sexual activity;

(b) The exploitative use of children in prostitution or other unlawful sexual practices;

(c) The exploitative use of children in pornographic performances and materials.

**Article 35**

States Parties shall take all appropriate national, bilateral and multilateral measures to prevent the abduction of, the sale of or traffic in children for any purpose or in any form.

**Article 36**

States Parties shall protect the child against all other forms of exploitation prejudicial to any aspects of the child's welfare.

## Article 37

States Parties shall ensure that:

(a) No child shall be subjected to torture or other cruel, inhuman or degrading treatment or punishment. Neither capital punishment nor life imprisonment without possibility of release shall be imposed for offences committed by persons below eighteen years of age;

(b) No child shall be deprived of his or her liberty unlawfully or arbitrarily. The arrest, detention or imprisonment of a child shall be in conformity with the law and shall be used only as a measure of last resort and for the shortest appropriate period of time;

(c) Every child deprived of liberty shall be treated with humanity and respect for the inherent dignity of the human person, and in a manner which takes into account the needs of persons of his or her age. In particular, every child deprived of liberty shall be separated from adults unless it is considered in the child's best interest not to do so and shall have the right to maintain contact with his or her family through correspondence and visits, save in exceptional circumstances;

(d) Every child deprived of his or her liberty shall have the right to prompt access to legal and other appropriate assistance, as well as the right to challenge the legality of the deprivation of his or her liberty before a court or other competent, independent and impartial authority, and to a prompt decision on any such action.

## Article 38

1. States Parties undertake to respect and to ensure respect for rules of international humanitarian law applicable to them in armed conflicts which are relevant to the child.

2. States Parties shall take all feasible measures to ensure that persons who have not attained the age of fifteen years do not take a direct part in hostilities.

3. States Parties shall refrain from recruiting any person who has not attained the age of fifteen years into their armed forces. In recruiting among those persons who have attained the age of fifteen years but who have not attained the age of eighteen years, States Parties shall endeavour to give priority to those who are oldest.

4. In accordance with their obligations under international humanitarian law to protect the civilian population in armed conflicts, States Parties shall take all feasible measures to ensure protection and care of children who are affected by an armed conflict.

**Article 39**

States Parties shall take all appropriate measures to promote physical and psychological recovery and social reintegration of a child victim of: any form of neglect, exploitation, or abuse; torture or any other form of cruel, inhuman or degrading treatment or punishment; or armed conflicts. Such recovery and reintegration shall take place in an environment which fosters the health, self-respect and dignity of the child.

**Article 40**

1. States Parties recognize the right of every child alleged as, accused of, or recognized as having infringed the penal law to be treated in a manner consistent with the promotion of the child's sense of dignity and worth, which reinforces the child's respect for the human rights and fundamental freedoms of others and which takes into account the child's age and the desirability of promoting the child's reintegration and the child's assuming a constructive role in society.

2. To this end, and having regard to the relevant provisions of international instruments, States Parties shall, in particular, ensure that:

(a) No child shall be alleged as, be accused of, or recognized as having infringed the penal law by reason of acts or omissions that were not prohibited by national or international law at the time they were committed;

(b) Every child alleged as or accused of having infringed the penal law has at least the following guarantees:

(i) To be presumed innocent until proven guilty according to law;

(ii) To be informed promptly and directly of the charges against him or her, and, if appropriate, through his or her parents or legal guardians, and to have legal or other appropriate assistance in the preparation and presentation of his or her defence;

(iii) To have the matter determined without delay by a competent, independent and impartial authority or judicial body in a fair hearing according to law, in the presence of legal or other appropriate assistance and, unless it is considered not to be in the best interest of the child, in particular, taking into account his or her age or situation, his or her parents or legal guardians;

(iv) Not to be compelled to give testimony or to confess guilt; to examine or have examined adverse witnesses and to obtain the participation and examination of witnesses on his or her behalf under conditions of equality;

(v) If considered to have infringed the penal law, to have this decision and any measures imposed in consequence thereof reviewed by a higher competent, independent and impartial authority or judicial body according to law;

(vi) To have the free assistance of an interpreter if the child cannot understand or speak the language used;

(vii) To have his or her privacy fully respected at all stages of the proceedings.

3. States Parties shall seek to promote the establishment of laws, procedures, authorities and institutions specifically applicable to children alleged as, accused of, or recognized as having infringed the penal law, and, in particular:

(a) The establishment of a minimum age below which children shall be presumed not to have the capacity to infringe the penal law;

(b) Whenever appropriate and desirable, measures for dealing with such children without resorting to judicial proceedings, providing that human rights and legal safeguards are fully respected. 4. A variety of dispositions, such as care, guidance and supervision orders; counselling; probation; foster care; education and vocational training programmes and other alternatives to institutional care shall be available to ensure that children are dealt with in a manner appropriate to their well-being and proportionate both to their circumstances and the offence.

**Article 41**

Nothing in the present Convention shall affect any provisions which are more conducive to the realization of the rights of the child and which may be contained in:

(a) The law of a State party; or

(b) International law in force for that State.

## PART II

**Article 42**

States Parties undertake to make the principles and provisions of the Convention widely known, by appropriate and active means, to adults and children alike.

**Article 43**

1. For the purpose of examining the progress made by States Parties in achieving the realization of the obligations undertaken in the present Convention, there shall be established a Committee on the Rights of the Child, which shall carry out the functions hereinafter provided.

2. The Committee shall consist of ten experts of high moral standing and recognized competence in the field covered by this Convention. The members of the Committee shall be elected by States Parties

from among their nationals and shall serve in their personal capacity, consideration being given to equitable geographical distribution, as well as to the principal legal systems.

3. The members of the Committee shall be elected by secret ballot from a list of persons nominated by States Parties. Each State Party may nominate one person from among its own nationals.

4. The initial election to the Committee shall be held no later than six months after the date of the entry into force of the present Convention and thereafter every second year. At least four months before the date of each election, the Secretary-General of the United Nations shall address a letter to States Parties inviting them to submit their nominations within two months. The Secretary-General shall subsequently prepare a list in alphabetical order of all persons thus nominated, indicating States Parties which have nominated them, and shall submit it to the States Parties to the present Convention.

5. The elections shall be held at meetings of States Parties convened by the Secretary-General at United Nations Headquarters. At those meetings, for which two thirds of States Parties shall constitute a quorum, the persons elected to the Committee shall be those who obtain the largest number of votes and an absolute majority of the votes of the representatives of States Parties present and voting.

6. The members of the Committee shall be elected for a term of four years. They shall be eligible for re-election if renominated. The term of five of the members elected at the first election shall expire at the end of two years; immediately after the first election, the names of these five members shall be chosen by lot by the Chairman of the meeting.

7. If a member of the Committee dies or resigns or declares that for any other cause he or she can no longer perform the duties of the Committee, the State Party which nominated the member shall appoint another expert from among its nationals to serve for the remainder of the term, subject to the approval of the Committee.

8. The Committee shall establish its own rules of procedure.

9. The Committee shall elect its officers for a period of two years.

10. The meetings of the Committee shall normally be held at United Nations Headquarters or at any other convenient place as determined by the Committee. The Committee shall normally meet annually. The duration of the meetings of the Committee shall be determined, and reviewed, if necessary, by a meeting of the States Parties to the present Convention, subject to the approval of the General Assembly.

11. The Secretary-General of the United Nations shall provide the necessary staff and facilities for the effective performance of the functions of the Committee under the present Convention.

12. With the approval of the General Assembly, the members of the Committee established under the present Convention shall receive emoluments from United Nations resources on such terms and conditions as the Assembly may decide.

**Article 44**

1. States Parties undertake to submit to the Committee, through the Secretary-General of the United Nations, reports on the measures they have adopted which give effect to the rights recognized herein and on the progress made on the enjoyment of those rights

(a) Within two years of the entry into force of the Convention for the State Party concerned;
(b) Thereafter every five years.

2. Reports made under the present article shall indicate factors and difficulties, if any, affecting the degree of fulfilment of the obligations under the present Convention. Reports shall also contain sufficient information to provide the Committee with a comprehensive understanding of the implementation of the Convention in the country concerned.

3. A State Party which has submitted a comprehensive initial report to the Committee need not, in its subsequent reports submitted in accordance with paragraph 1 (b) of the present article, repeat basic information previously provided.

4. The Committee may request from States Parties further information relevant to the implementation of the Convention.

5. The Committee shall submit to the General Assembly, through the Economic and Social Council, every two years, reports on its activities.

6. States Parties shall make their reports widely available to the public in their own countries.

**Article 45**

In order to foster the effective implementation of the Convention and to encourage international co-operation in the field covered by the Convention:

(a) The specialized agencies, the United Nations Children's Fund, and other United Nations organs shall be entitled to be represented at the consideration of the implementation of such provisions of the present Convention as fall within the scope of their mandate. The Committee may invite the specialized agencies, the United Nations Children's Fund and other competent bodies as it may consider appropriate to provide expert advice on the implementation of the Convention in areas falling within the scope of their respective mandates. The Committee may invite the specialized agencies, the United Nations Children's Fund, and other United Nations organs to submit reports on the implementation of the Convention in areas falling within the scope of their activities;

(b) The Committee shall transmit, as it may consider appropriate, to the specialized agencies, the United Nations Children's Fund and other competent bodies, any reports from States Parties that contain a request, or indicate a need, for technical advice or assistance, along with the Committee's observations and suggestions, if any, on these requests or indications;

(c) The Committee may recommend to the General Assembly to request the Secretary-General to undertake on its behalf studies on specific issues relating to the rights of the child;

(d) The Committee may make suggestions and general recommendations based on information received pursuant to articles 44 and 45 of the present Convention. Such suggestions and general recommendations shall be transmitted to any State Party concerned and reported to the General Assembly, together with comments, if any, from States Parties.

## PART III

### Article 46

The present Convention shall be open for signature by all States.

### Article 47

The present Convention is subject to ratification. Instruments of ratification shall be deposited with the Secretary-General of the United Nations.

### Article 48

The present Convention shall remain open for accession by any State. The instruments of accession shall be deposited with the Secretary-General of the United Nations.

### Article 49

1. The present Convention shall enter into force on the thirtieth day following the date of deposit with the Secretary-General of the United Nations of the twentieth instrument of ratification or accession.

2. For each State ratifying or acceding to the Convention after the deposit of the twentieth instrument of ratification or accession, the Convention shall enter into force on the thirtieth day after the deposit by such State of its instrument of ratification or accession.

### Article 50

1. Any State Party may propose an amendment and file it with the Secretary-General of the United Nations. The Secretary-General

shall thereupon communicate the proposed amendment to States Parties, with a request that they indicate whether they favour a conference of States Parties for the purpose of considering and voting upon the proposals. In the event that, within four months from the date of such communication, at least one third of the States Parties favour such a conference, the Secretary-General shall convene the conference under the auspices of the United Nations. Any amendment adopted by a majority of States Parties present and voting at the conference shall be submitted to the General Assembly for approval.

2. An amendment adopted in accordance with paragraph 1 of the present article shall enter into force when it has been approved by the General Assembly of the United Nations and accepted by a two-thirds majority of States Parties.

3. When an amendment enters into force, it shall be binding on those States Parties which have accepted it, other States Parties still being bound by the provisions of the present Convention and any earlier amendments which they have accepted.

**Article 51**

1. The Secretary-General of the United Nations shall receive and circulate to all States the text of reservations made by States at the time of ratification or accession.

2. A reservation incompatible with the object and purpose of the present Convention shall not be permitted.

3. Reservations may be withdrawn at any time by notification to that effect addressed to the Secretary-General of the United Nations, who shall then inform all States. Such notification shall take effect on the date on which it is received by the Secretary-General

**Article 52**

A State Party may denounce the present Convention by written notification to the Secretary-General of the United Nations.

Denunciation becomes effective one year after the date of receipt of the notification by the Secretary-General.

**Article 53**

The Secretary-General of the United Nations is designated as the depositary of the present Convention.

**Article 54**

The original of the present Convention, of which the Arabic, Chinese, English, French, Russian and Spanish texts are equally authentic, shall be deposited with the Secretary-General of the United Nations.

IN WITNESS THEREOF the undersigned plenipotentiaries, being duly authorized thereto by their respective governments, have signed the present Convention.

# Draft School Child Rights Policy

This Appendix presents some ideas for a Policy that could be used by schools who wish to show that they recognize and will do their best to implement the United Nations Convention on the Rights of the Child (UNCRC). In the UK, such a policy is not a statutory policy, and some schools may prefer to call it a guideline.

---

## [insert name] SCHOOL

## Children Rights Policy

| **Status** | Proposed | **Approval** | Board of Governors |
|---|---|---|---|
| **Maintenance** | [committee responsible] | **Role(s) responsible** | [child rights champion] |
| **Date effective** | [date adopted] | **Date of last review** | [date of last review] |
| **Date of next review** | [date for review] | **Date withdrawn** | [date if withdrawn] |

# CHILDREN RIGHTS POLICY

Overall, we aim to create a School environment in which each member of the community knows about the rights of everyone, and always acts to ensure that those rights are made available to everyone, to the greatest extent possible. Each member of the community must be capable of being relied upon to respect each other's strengths and weaknesses.

## Purpose

The UK ratified the United Nations Convention on the Rights of the Child (UNCRC) in 1991 (UNGA, 1989). As a result, the UK has assumed a set of legal responsibilities.

Not all of the provisions of the UNCRC apply to education or schools. However, some of them do, and this Policy provides a brief summary of how the School meets the requirements of the UNCRC.

Many parts of this policy are derived directly from the UNCRC.

## Principles

Several principles arise from the UNCRC with respect to education.

- Certain rights impact a child's school environment
- There are other rights that have little direct impact on a child's school environment
- There are very few absolute rights; many rights require the rights of a child to be balanced with the rights of others
- Countries that ratify or acceded to the Convention are taking on legally binding responsibilities that can be used in UK courts to help with interpretation

Several rights arise from the UNCRC with respect to education. These are the subject matter of this Policy:

- child protection and safeguarding
- education rights

- freedom of expression
- freedom of thought, conscience, and religion
- knowledge of UNCRC
- rights of assembly and association
- rights of privacy, family life, and reputation
- right to challenge punishment and detention
- right to freedom from exploitation
- special educational needs

This policy is related to other policies and the general school curriculum, which have their own contributions to meeting the requirements of the UNCRC.

## Child Protection and Safeguarding

The School has developed and adopted several policies for Child Protection and Safeguarding. See the section on Related Policies for the names of the various policies.

## Education Rights

The provision of primary, secondary, further, and higher education in the UK satisfies the rights that these should be available.

We will make pupils aware of vocational, academic and combined educational paths. We provide appropriate vocational education in addition to more classical academic education. It is acknowledged that this is a systemic weakness in UK schools. We will do our best to correct this.

The school's Attendance policy explains how we support that right.

The School's Behaviour Policy sets out what is expected of children at the school. All children have rights with respect to discipline in an educational setting, there not only does each child have such rights, but each child also has responsibilities to behave in a way that does not adversely affect other children.

School discipline is administered in a manner consistent with the child's human dignity and in conformity with the UNCRC

The school curriculum and general school ecology are designed to encourage:

- The development of each child's personality, talents and mental and physical abilities to their fullest potential;
- The development of respect for human rights and fundamental freedoms, and for the principles enshrined in the Charter of the United Nations;
- The development of respect for the child's parents, his or her own cultural identity, language and values, for the national values of the country in which the child is living, the country from which he or she may originate, and for civilizations different from his or her own.

We prepare children for:

- The preparation of the child for responsible life in a free society, in the spirit of understanding, peace, tolerance, equality of sexes, and friendship among all peoples, ethnic, national and religious groups and persons of indigenous origin;
- The development of respect for the natural environment.

**Freedom of Expression**

Each child is encouraged to form his or her own views and has the right to express those views freely in all matters affecting the child, the views of the child being given due weight in accordance with the age and maturity of the child. Freedom of expression may be restricted at some times and in some situations, for the purpose of maintaining an ordered school environment.

Each child has the right to freedom of expression; this right shall include freedom to seek, receive and impart information and ideas of all kinds, regardless of frontiers, either orally, in writing or in print, in the form of art, or through any other media of the child's choice.

The school provides facilities for children to express any concerns they have about any aspect of their school or educational situation. Concerns may be expressed anonymously. The school governors put in place mechanisms to consider all concerns expressed by pupils and to ensure that do child suffers any detriment from expressing a concern, as long as the concern is expressed in good faith and is not malicious.

## Freedom of Thought, Conscience, and Religion

Each child has freedom of thought, conscience and religion.

## Knowledge of UNCRC

The School will display copies of the UNCRC in include discussion of it in the school curriculum.

## Rights of Assembly and Association

Children in the school have rights of freedom of association and freedom of peaceful assembly, subject only to the maintenance of good order in the school. If children wish to meet to discuss some topic, the school will do its best to provide an appropriate room for such discussions.

## Rights of Privacy, Family Life, and Reputation

No child shall be subjected to arbitrary or unlawful interference with his or her privacy, family, home or correspondence, nor to unlawful attacks on his or her honour and reputation.

## Right to Challenge Punishment and Detention

Every child who is to be punished or given a school detention has the normal rights of natural justice to a satisfactory explanation of reasons and may challenge any facts leading to the punishment or detention. The school has a panel that the child can appeal to, for the purposes of determining facts and punishment, and the school has an independent and impartial panel who can hear any subsequent appeal by a child. The child has the right to be represented in any such hearings.

## Right to Freedom from Exploitation

The school provides each child with appropriate rest and leisure, to engage in play and recreational activities appropriate to the age of the child and to participate freely in cultural life and the arts.

The school protects children from economic exploitation either in school, or by including information about exploitation in the curriculum.

Children are not asked to perform any work that is likely to be hazardous or to interfere with the child's education, or to be harmful to the child's health or physical, mental, spiritual, moral or social development.

The school takes steps to protect children from all forms of exploitation and abuse. The school does not permit any activities by anyone which support or condone any unlawful sexual activity.

## Special Educational Needs

The School has policies related to special educational needs to ensure that all children, when in school, enjoy a full and decent life, in conditions which ensure dignity, promote self-reliance and facilitate the child's active participation in the community.

## Related Policies

There are several other school policies related to this Policy. They give more detail on a range of point.

[include a list of related policies here. Each school will have developed its own set of policies. These may be separate policies, or a much smaller number of synoptic policies. Some Policy names that have been encountered in schools, include:

Accessibility
Attendance
Behaviour
Charging and Remissions
Child Protection Procedures
Code of Conduct
Confidentiality
Curriculum
Dealing with Allegations
Disability Equality
Discipline

Equal Opportunities
Exclusion
Fairness and Dignity at School
Fairness and Dignity at Work
Gender and Sex Equality
Grievance
Health and Safety
Home-School Agreements
Inclusion
Intimate Care
Most Able and Talented
Performance Management
Physical Intervention
Race Equality
Restraint
Safeguarding
Sex Education
Special Educational Needs
Violence at Work
Whistleblowing

...
...]

# Wikipedia Articles

There are several Wikipedia articles relevant directly or indirectly to the subject matter of this book.

Do not let reservations by many writers and academics about the value of Wikipedia get in the way of making good use of these articles. Many are replete with references to good sources and have clearly been written by people with excellent knowledge and experience.

It was tempting to include some of these articles here, but that temptation has been resisted. They are freely available, and doubtless they will evolve over time to incorporate new experience, legislation, and practices. Table A.1 offers a sample list of topics, and URLs to them (working in July 2012).

Reservations about Wikipedia articles usually centre around the issue of peer review.

Keep in mind that Wikipedia is an encyclopedia. As such, it does not present new and original research; it presents topics for which there are independent verifiable sources for the points being made. Indeed, it is a condition of putting a new article into Wikipedia that it is not original research.

The review process for Wikipedia is thorough. It is not possible simply to write anything about a subject and have it added to Wikipedia; there is a thorough review process.

Hesitations over using Wikipedia as a source are understandable only in the sense that the articles are not original research. However, there is no good reason not to use Wikipedia as a source of summaries of key issues related to a subject.

| Topic | URL |
|---|---|
| **Abuse** | http://en.wikipedia.org/wiki/Abuse |
| **Aggression** | http://en.wikipedia.org/wiki/Aggression |
| **Bullying** | http://en.wikipedia.org/wiki/Bullying |
| **Caning** | http://en.wikipedia.org/wiki/Caning |
| **Child Abuse** | http://en.wikipedia.org/wiki/Child_abuse |

| Topic | URL |
|---|---|
| **Child protection** | http://en.wikipedia.org/wiki/Child_protection |
| **Conflict tactics scale** | http://en.wikipedia.org/wiki/Conflict_tactics_scale |
| **Corporal punishment** | http://en.wikipedia.org/wiki/Corporal_punishment |
| **Covert Aggression** | see relational aggression |
| **Emotional Abuse Psychological Abuse Mental Abuse** | http://en.wikipedia.org/wiki/Psychological_abuse<br><br>[emotional abuse redirects to Psychological Abuse in Wikipedia] |
| **Gaslighting** | http://en.wikipedia.org/wiki/Gaslighting |
| **Harassment** | http://en.wikipedia.org/wiki/Harassment |
| **Neglect** | http://en.wikipedia.org/wiki/Neglect |
| **Relational aggression** | http://en.wikipedia.org/wiki/Relational_aggression |
| **Sexual abuse** | http://en.wikipedia.org/wiki/Sexual_abuse |
| **Teacher Abuse** | http://en.wikipedia.org/wiki/Teacher_abuse [redirected from Bullying in teaching] |
| **Verbal abuse** | http://en.wikipedia.org/wiki/Verbal_abuse |

**Table A.1. Sample of relevant Wikipedia articles**

# References

Archard, D. (2009) 'Every Child's Rights Matter' in Broadhurst, K., Grover, C., and Jamieson, J. (eds.) *Critical Perspectives on Safeguarding Children*, Chichester: Wiley-Blackwell pp39-53.

Benbenishty, R., and Astor, R.A. (2005) *School Violence in Context - Culture, Neighborhood, Family, School, and Gender*, Oxford: Oxford University Press.

Berlin, L.J., Ispa, J.M., Fine, M.A., Malone, P.S., Brooks-Gunn, J., Brady-Smith, C., Ayoub, C., and Bai, Y. (2009) "Correlates and Consequences of Spanking and Verbal Punishment for Low-Income White, African American, and Mexican American Toddlers" in *Child Development* 80(5) pp1403-1420.

Broadhurst, K. (2009) 'Safeguarding Children through Parenting Support: How Does *Every Parent Matter*?' in Broadhurst, K., Grover, C., and Jamieson, J. (eds.) *Critical Perspectives on Safeguarding Children*, Chichester: Wiley-Blackwell pp 111-130.

Broadhurst, K., Grover, C., and Jamieson, J. (eds.) (2009a) *Critical Perspectives on Safeguarding Children*, Chichester: Wiley-Blackwell.

Broadhurst, K., Grover, C., and Jamieson, J. (2009b) 'Introduction: Safeguarding Children?' in Broadhurst, K., Grover, C., and Jamieson, J. (eds.) *Critical Perspectives on Safeguarding Children*, Chichester: Wiley-Blackwell pp1-15.

CDD (2011) *Introduction to DD* [domestic discipline]: *basic history and concepts*. [available at: http://www.christiandomesticdiscipline.com/introdd.html - July 2012].

Charles, C.M. (2002) *Building Classroom Discipline*, Boston, MA: Allyn and Bacon.

Darnton, G. and Giacoletto, S. (1992) *Information in the Enterprise*, Burlington, MA: Digital Press.

DES (1989) *Discipline in Schools [The Elton Report]*, London: Her Majesty's Stationery Office

DCSF (2010) *Working Together to Safeguard Children: A guide to inter-agency working to safeguard and promote the welfare of children*, London: Department for Children, Schools, and Families. [Available at: https://www.education.gov.uk/publications/eOrderingDownload/00305-2010DOM-EN-v3.pdf - July 2012].

DfES (2003a) *Keeping children safe: The Government's response to The Victoria Climbié Inquiry Report and Joint Chief Inspectors' Report Safeguarding Children*, London: Department for Education and Skills.

DfES (2003b). *Every child matters [Green Paper]*, London: Department for Education and Skills.

DfES (2004a). "*Every Child Matters: Change for Children*", DfES, (ed.). London: Department for Education and Skills.

DfES (2004b). "*Every child matters: next steps*", DfES, (ed.). London: The Stationery Office:

DfES (2007a) *Safeguarding Children and Safer Recruitment in Education,* London: Department for Education and Skills. [Available at: https://www.education.gov.uk/publications/eOrderingDownload/Final%206836-SafeGuard.Chd%20bkmk.pdf - July 2012].

DfES (2007b) *Every Parent Matters,* London: Department for Education and Skills.

Erickson, M.F., and Egeland, B. (1987) " A Developmental View of the Psychological Consequences of Maltreatment" in School Psychology Review 16(2) pp156-168.

Field, J.E., Kolbert, J.B., Crothers, L.M., and Hughes, T.L. (2009) *Understanding Girl Bullying and What to Do About It: Strategies to Help Heal the Divide,* Thousand Oaks, CA: Corwen

Fitzpatrick, C. (2009) 'Looked After Children and the Criminal Justice System' in Broadhurst, K., Grover, C., and Jamieson, J. (eds.) *Critical Perspectives on Safeguarding Children*, Chichester: Wiley-Blackwell pp 211-227.

Gove, P.B. (ed.) (2002) *Webster's Third New International Dictionary of the English Language Unabridged,* Springfield MA: Merriam-Webster Inc.

Grover, C. (2009) 'Child Poverty' in Broadhurst, K., Grover, C., and Jamieson, J. (eds.) *Critical Perspectives on Safeguarding Children,* Chichester: Wiley-Blackwell pp55-72.

Halpern, D. (2005) *Social Capital,* Cambridge: Polity Press.

Higgins, S., Kokotsaki, D. & Coe, R.J. (2011). *Toolkit of Strategies to Improve Learning: Summary for Schools Spending the Pupil Premium.* London: Sutton Trust.

Hill, M. and Hopkins, P. (2009) 'Safeguarding Children Who Are Refugees or Asylum Seekers: Managing Multiple Scales of Legislation and Policy' in Broadhurst, K., Grover, C., and Jamieson, J. (eds.) *Critical Perspectives on Safeguarding Children*, Chichester: Wiley-Blackwell pp 229-246.

Hofstede, G., Hofstede, G.J., and Minkov, M. (2010) *Cultures and Organizations: Software of the Mind: intercultural cooperation and its importance for survival,* New York: McGraw Hill.

Hopkins, G. (2007) "What have we learned? Child death scandals since 1944", Community Care 11th January 2007, www: http://www.communitycare.co.uk/Articles/11/01/2007/102713/What-have-we-learned-Child-death-scandals-since-1944.htm [accessed July 2012].

Hyman, I.A. (1990) *Reading Writing and the Hickory Stick - The Appalling Story of Physical and Psychological Abuse in American Schools,* Lexington, MA: Lexington Books

Hyman, I.A. (1997) *The Case Against Spanking - How to Discipline Your Child Without Hitting*, San Francisco: Josey-Bass Publishers.

Hyman, I.A. and Snook, P.A. (1999) *Dangerous Schools - What we Can Do About the Physical and Emotional Abuse of Our Children*, San Francisco: Jossey-Bass Publishers.

Jamieson, J. (2009) 'In Search of Youth Justice' in Broadhurst, K., Grover, C., and Jamieson, J. (eds.) *Critical Perspectives on Safeguarding Children*, Chichester: Wiley-Blackwell pp 189-209.

Knowles, M. S. (1973). *The adult learner: A neglected species.* Houston, TX: Gulf Publishing Company.

Kohlberg, L. (1981). *Essays on Moral Development, Vol. I: The Philosophy of Moral Development*, San Francisco, CA: Harper & Row.

Kohn, A. (1993) *Punished by Rewards—The Trouble With Gold Stars, Incentive Plans, A's, Praise, and Other Bribes,* Boston, MA: Houghton Mifflin Co.

Laming, W.H. (2003) *The Victoria Climbié Inquiry: Report of an Inquiry by Lord Laming,* London: HMSO.

League of Nations (1924) *Geneva Declaration of the Rights of the Child,* Geneva: League of Nations. [available at: http://www.unicef.org/vietnam/01_-_Declaration_of_Geneva_1924.PDF - July 2012]

McEachern, A.G., Aluede, O., and Kenny, M.C. (2008) "Emotional Abuse in the Classroom: Implications and Interventions for Counselors" in *Journal of Counseling & Development* Vol 86 Winter 2008.

Mezirow, J. (1981) "A Critical Theory of Adult Learning and Education" in *Adult Education, 32(1),* pp3-24.

Morris, D. (1994) *The Human Animal,* London: BBC Books.

Nesbit, W. (1991) *Mutilation of the Spirit: The Educational Context of Emotional Abuse,* St. John's, NF: Memorial University of Newfoundland.

Nesbit, W.C., and, Philpott, David F. (2002) "Confronting Subtle Emotional Abuse in Classrooms" in *Guidance Counselling* 17(2) pp32-38.

OCC (2006) *Bullying Today: A Report by the Office of the Children's Commissioner, with Recommendations and Links to Practitioner Tools,* London: Office of the Children's Commissioner

OCC (2010) *About the Office of the Children's Commissioner,* London: Office of the Children's Commissioner.

OCC (2012), *Office of the Children's Commissioner: Annual Report and Financial Statements for 2011-2012,* London: Office of the Children's Commissioner.

OED (2009) *Oxford English Dictionary Second edition on CD-ROM Version 4.0,* Oxford: Oxford University Press.

Olweus, D. (1993) *Bullying at School: What We Know and What We Can Do,* Chichester: Wiley-Blackwell.

Olweus, D., and Limber, S. P. (2007). *Olweus Bullying Prevention Program Teacher Guide,* Center City, MN: Hazelden. [includes DVD and CD]

Palmer, G. (2011) *UK Underage Pregnancies,* WWW: The Poverty Site [available at: http://www.poverty.org.uk/24/index.shtml - accessed July 2012].

Parton, N. (2004) "From Maria Colwell to Victoria Climbié : Reflections on a Generation of Public Inquiries into Child Abuse" in *Child Abuse Review* (2004), 13 (2), pp80-94). [available at: http://www.gptsw.net/papers/clwlclmbi.pdf - July 2012].

Parton, Nigel (2011) "The increasing length and complexity of central government guidance about child abuse in England: 1974-2010". Discussion Paper. University of Huddersfield, Huddersfield. (Unpublished) [available at http://eprints.hud.ac.uk/9906 - July 2012]./

Paylor, I. (2009) ''Be Healthy': Drugs, Alcohol and Safeguarding Children' in Broadhurst, K., Grover, C., and Jamieson, J. (eds.) *Critical Perspectives on Safeguarding Children*, Chichester: Wiley-Blackwell pp 171-187.

Peckover, S. (2009) ''Health' and Safeguarding Children: An 'Expansionary Proejct' or Good Practice'?' in Broadhurst, K., Grover, C., and Jamieson, J. (eds.) *Critical Perspectives on Safeguarding Children*, Chichester: Wiley-Blackwell pp 149-169.

Pithouse, A. and Broadhurst, K. (2009) 'The Common Assessment Framework: Effective Innovation for Children and Young People with'Additional Needs' or Simply More Technical Hype?' in Broadhurst, K., Grover, C., and Jamieson, J. (eds.) *Critical Perspectives on Safeguarding Children*, Chichester: Wiley-Blackwell pp73-91.

Prensky, M. (2006) *Don't Bother Me Mom—I'm Learning! : how computer and video games are preparing your kids for 21st century success and how you can help!*, St. Paul, MN: Paragon House.

Sawyer, M. (2003). "Sex is not just for grown-ups" London: The Observer. 2 November 2003.

Smith, P.K., Morita Y., Junger-Tas, J., Olweus, D., Catalano, R., and Slee, P. (eds.) (1999) *The Nature of School Bullying: A cross-national perspective*, London: Routledge.

Straus, M.A., and Field, C.J. (2003) "Psychological Aggression by American Parents: National Data on Prevalence, Chronicity, and Severity" in Journal of Marriage and Family, 65 (November 2003) pp795-808.

Taylor, C. (2009) 'Safeguarding Children: Historical Context and Current Landscape' in Broadhurst, K., Grover, C., and Jamieson, J. (eds.) *Critical Perspectives on Safeguarding Children*, Chichester: Wiley-Blackwell pp17-38.

UN (1978) United Nations Declaration of the Rights of the Child: Plain Language Version, United Nations Cyber School Bus. [available at: http://www.un.org/cyberschoolbus/humanrights/resources/plainchild.asp - July 2012].

UNGA (1989) *Convention on the Rights of the Child*, New York: United Nations General Assembly. [available via general discussion at http://www.unicef.org/crc/; English edition at: http://www2.ohchr.org/english/law/pdf/crc.pdf. July 2012]

UNICEF (2007) *Child poverty in perspective: An overview of child well-being in rich countries, Innocenti Report Card* 7, Florence: Innocenti Research Centre,

UNICEF (2011) *Child well-being in the UK, Spain and Sweden: The role of inequality and materialism,* WWW: http://www.unicef.org.uk/Documents/Publications/UNICEFIpsosMori_childwellbeing_reportsummary.pdf [accessed July 2012]

UNICEF (2012) *Measuring Child Poverty: New league tables of child poverty in the world's rich countries: Innocenti Report Card 10*, Florence: UNICEF Innocenti Research Centre

USDOJ (2012) Domestic Violence, US Department of Justice available at: http://www.ovw.usdoj.gov/domviolence.htm [accessed 2012-07-08].

Vachss, A. (1994) " You Carry the Cure In Your Own Heart", in Parade Magazine, August 28, 1994 (available at: http://www.vachss.com/av_dispatches/disp_9408_a.html) [accessed 2012-07-08].

Volpe, R. (1980) *The Maltreatment of School Aged Children,* Lexington Books.

Warin, J. (2009) 'Safeguarding Children's Well-being within Educational Settings: A Critical Review of Inclusion Strategies' in Broadhurst, K., Grover, C., and Jamieson, J. (eds.) *Critical Perspectives on Safeguarding Children*, Chichester: Wiley-Blackwell pp 131-147.

White, S. (2009) 'Arguing the Case in Safeguarding' in Broadhurst, K., Grover, C., and Jamieson, J. (eds.) *Critical Perspectives on Safeguarding Children*, Chichester: Wiley-Blackwell pp93-109.

Wilson, K., and James, A. (eds.) (2007) *The Child Protection Handbook - The practitioner's guide to safeguarding children* (3rd ed.), Edinburgh: Baillière Tindall.

# Index

## A

abuse 6, 23
  dictionary definitions 11
  in Wikipedia 137
  meanings 23
abuser motivations 19
abusers
  predictors 21
adult learning 31
age of consent 3
aggression
  covert 29
  indirect 29
  in Wikipedia 137
  psychological 14
  relational 30
  social 30
Albert, L. 33
Aluede, O. 14, 21, 33, 141
American parents 17
andragogy 31
anonymity 66
anxiety induction 36
Archard, D. 58, 139
Astor, R.A. 22, 30, 139
attainment
  teaching, and 28
Ayoub, C. 139

## B

bad classroom experiences 92
Bai, Y. 139
behaviour
  prejudicial 36
behaviours and risks
  UK bottom of the league 56
being healthy 52
Benbenishty, R. 22, 30, 139
Berlin, L.J. 17, 22, 23, 26, 139
blended learning 7, 28, 31
bored children 29
Brady-Smith, C. 139
Broadhurst, K. 55, 58, 139, 142
Brooks-Gunn, J. 139
bullying 5, 18, 29
  and abuse 6
  by children 6
  by teachers 6
  impact on a child 41
  in Wikipedia 137
bullying in teaching
  in Wikipedia 138
bully research 30

## C

caning
  introduced for child protection 39
  in Wikipedia 137
Canter, L. 33
Canter, M. 33
Catalano, R. 142
Charles, C.M. 33, 139
child abuse 1
  in Wikipedia 137
child awareness of learning 31
child care 29
child feedback contexts 66
child learning 31
child mental health, 44
child obedience 33
child protection 1, 7, 39–41
  in Wikipedia 138
  multi-agency 40
  requiring child punishment 39
  scope 40
  training 1
  under-age sexual activity, and 45
children
  feeling happy and safe 41
  holistic development 41
  views taken into account 53
Children Act 2004 8, 43, 44, 49
Children Rights Policy 8, 10, 59, 129–135
  principles 130
  related policies 134
children rights policy for schools 64–

65
curriculum adjustments 64
Children's Commissioner 8
general functions 52
UNCRC, and 58
children's services authorities 44
responsibilities 52
child respect for teachers 31
classroom abuse 35–37
prevalence 19
classroom behaviour 7
demeaning 36
destabilizing 36
discriminating 36
distancing 37
diverse 37
dominating 36
classroom discipline 32–33
classroom ecology 32
classroom environment 28
modern urban environment 34
classroom experiences
bad 92
good 91
ugly 92
Coe, R.J. 34, 140
cognitive ability 36
Coloroso, B. 33
Common Assessment Framework 58
community breakdown 29, 34, 57
confidentiality 2, 66
Conflict Tactics Scale
in Wikipedia 138
confrontational situations 23
consumerism 29
cooperative classroom environment 34
corporal punishment 3, 16
by parents 3
defined 25
definition 4, 93
institutionalized 3
in UK schools 3
in Wikipedia 138
scope 4
sexual gratification from 4
US 4
without hitting or striking 7
corporal punishment without physical pain
definition 93
corporal punishment with physical pain
definition 93
covert aggression 29
in Wikipedia 138
cross-cultural research 22
Crothers, L.M. 140
cultural norms
abuse, and 21
Curwin, R. 33

## D

Darnton, G. 31, 139
DCSF 13, 43, 139
debate 23
defence 23, 24
demeaning behaviour
child perspective 78–79
teacher perspective 70
demeaning classroom behaviour 36
denigration 18, 36
Department for Children, Schools and Families
see DCSF
Department for Education and Skills
see DfES 42
Department of Education and Science
see DES
deprivation punishment 24
DES 30
destabilizing behaviour
child perspective 85–86
teacher perspective 73
destabilizing classroom behaviour 36
Deuteronomy 2
DfES 42, 43, 49, 51, 139–140
diminished respect for teacher 17
disagreement 23
discipline 33
discriminating behaviour
child perspective 80–82
teacher perspective 71
discriminating classroom behaviour 36

distancing behaviour
  child perspective 87–88
  teacher perspective 74
distancing classroom behaviour 37
diverse behaviour
  child perspective 89
  teacher perspective 75
diverse classroom behaviour 37
dominating behaviour 20
  child perspective 83–84
  teacher perspective 72
dominating classroom behaviour 36
Dreikers, R. 33


## E


ECHR 46
ECM 1, 8, 43, 49–66
  as rhetoric 49
  history 49–50
  outcomes and aims 50
economic well-being 52
educational theory 30
education rights 62–63, 131–132
Educator-Induced Post traumatic Stress Disorder'
  see EIPTSD
Egeland, B. 20, 140
EIPTSD 20
Elementary Education Act 1870 30
Elton Report 30
embarrassment 36
emotion 15
  dictionary definitions 11
emotional abuse 1, 7, 15
  definition 12–13, 14, 16, 93
  effects of 20, 44
  forms of 16–17, 35
  in the classroom 7
  in Wikipedia 138
  perpetrators 29
  prevalence 19
  received by teachers 20
emotional abuse in the classroom
  lack of material 41
  weakness in safeguarding 41
emotional abusers 19
emotional support
  lacking 37
emotional well-being
  statutory duty 44
enjoying and achieving 52
Erickson, M.F. 20, 140
eroticism 40
European Convention on Human Rights
  see ECHR
Every Child Matters
  see ECM
Every Parent Matters 57
exclusion 25
extended families 29


## F


family and peer relationships
  UK bottom of the league 56
family dynamics 21
family-oriented values 55
feeling happy and safe 41
Field, C.J. 13, 14, 17, 22, 142
Field, J.E. 29, 30, 140
Fine, M.A. 139
Fitzpatrick, C. 57, 65, 140
freedom of expression 60, 132
  implementation 65
freedom of thought, conscience and religion 61, 133


## G


gaslighting 18, 138
Geneva Declaration of the Rights of the Child 95
Giacoletto, S. 31, 139
Ginott, H. 33
Glasser, W. 33
Glenn, H. 33
good classroom experiences 91
Gordon, T. 33
gossip 19
Gove, P.B. 12, 25, 140
government initiatives 57
government policy
  focus on individuals and families 57

ignores socioeconomic norms and rhetoric 57
gratification 16
Grover, C. 55, 57, 139, 140, 141, 142, 143

## H

Halpern, D. 29, 140
hand
  punishment of 39
harassment 5
  in Wikipedia 138
Higgins, S. 34, 140
high profile cases 40
Hill, M. 59, 140
Hofstede, G. 22, 140
Hofstede, G.J. 22, 140
Hopkins, G. 51, 140
Hopkins, P. 59, 140
Hughes, T.L. 140
Human Rights Act 1998 59
humiliation 18, 36
Hyman, I.A. 3, 4, 14, 20, 24, 30, 140

## I

iatrogenic definition of emotional abuse 35
ignoring 18
inclusion
  resistance not deviancy 55
Indirect aggression 29
individualism 55
inequality 56
insults 18
intermediation
  new technology and media 31
intervention 14, 57
intimidation 36
isolation 25, 37
Ispa, J.M. 139

## J

James, A. 14, 41, 51, 143
Jamieson, J. 55, 57, 139, 140, 141, 142, 143
Jones, F.H. 33
Junger-Tas, J. 142

## K

Kagan, S. 33
Kenny, M.C. 14, 21, 33, 141
knowledge of UNCRC 64, 133
Knowles, M. S. 31, 141
know what Your schoolchildren really think 65–67
Kohlberg, L. 26, 141
Kohn, A. 33, 141
Kokotsaki, D. 34, 140
Kolbert, J.B. 140
Kounin, J. 33
Kyle, P. 33

## L

Laming Report 51
Laming, W.H. 51, 141
League of Nations 95, 141
Learning and Skills Act 2000 53
Limber, S.P. 5, 30, 141
local authority 53
local education authorities 53
looked after children 61
Lott, L. 33

## M

making a positive contribution 52
Malone, P.S. 139
materialism 55
McEachern, A.G. 14, 21, 33, 141
Mendler, A. 33
mental abuse 20
  in Wikipedia 138
mental illness 21
Mezirow, J. 31, 141
Minkov, M. 22, 140
modern technology and media
  effects of 31
moral development 7, 26
Morita Y. 142
Morris, D. 34, 141

## N

name-calling 18
nationality
as a proxy for culture 22
National Student Survey 65
neglect
in Wikipedia 138
Nelsen, J. 33
Nesbit, W.C. 13, 35–37, 36, 69–75, 77, 141
new technology and media 31
non-corporal punishment 26
nuclear families 29
nuclear family 57

## O

OED 11, 25, 141
Office of the Children's Commissioner 30, 54, 58, 141
Olweus, D. 5, 30, 141, 142
Oxford English Dictionary
see OED

## P

paddle 4
pain
psychological 15
Palmer, G. 45, 141
parenting 55
Parton, N. 51, 68, 142
PAST 35, 69–75
Paylor, I. 58, 142
Peckover, S. 58, 142
pedagogy 31
personal gratification 55
personality
abusers, and 19
Personal, Social, and Health Education
see PSHE
Philpott, D.F. 36, 141
physical abuse 1
emotional abuse, and 16
in schools 4
received by teachers 20
Pithouse, A. 58, 142
post traumatic stress disorder
see PTSD
power imbalance 19
power imbalance situations 19
prejudicial behaviour 36
Prensky, M. 34, 141
preventative disciplinary procedure 25
definition 93
regulated 27
problem-centred learning 31
procedure
punishment 24
retaliation 24
retribution 24
Protection from Harassment Act 1997 5
PSHE 54
psychological abuse 20
impact on a child 41
in Wikipedia 138
received by teachers 20
Psychological Abuse Scale for Teachers
see PAST
psychological aggression 14
as abuse 14
psychological consequences of maltreatment 20
psychological maltreatment
definition 14
PTSD 20
punishment 23, 39
abuse, and 7, 23
corporal without physical pain 25
corporal with physical pain 25
definition 24, 93
deprivation 25
is it abusive? 40
non-corporal 25
physical 7
verbal 7, 23
punishment in schools
policy formulation 27
pupil self-evaluation 9, 36, 77–90
putdowns 18

## R

race 36
Redl, F. 33

rejection 37
relational aggression 30
in Wikipedia 138
sex differences 30
relevant partners 44, 53
religious norms
abuse, and 21
restraint 23, 24
retaliation 7, 23, 24
definition 93
retribution 7, 24
definition 94
ridicule 18
rights of assembly and association 61, 133
rights of privacy, family life, and reputation 61, 133
right to challenge punishment and detentions 64, 133
right to cultural etc., participation 63
right to freedom from economic etc. exploitation 63, 133
right to freedom from sexual exploitation 64, 133
R v G [2008] UKHL 37 46

## S

sadism 40
safeguarding 7, 41–46
definition 42
Shared Objectives 42
statutory guidance 42
training 1
safer recruitment 1, 7, 46–47
sarcasm 18
Sawyer, M. 2, 45, 141
Scale of Subtle Emotional Abuse
see SSEA
scolding 26
Scott, S. 33
self-control 32
self-directedness 31
self-esteem 44
lowering 36
self-evaluation
teacher 35–37
self-indulgence 29
selfishness 29
SEN 62, 134
sex 36
sexual abuse 1, 45
in Wikipedia 138
sexual abusers 19
sexual activity 2
under-age 45
underage 2
Sexual Offences Act 2000 45
Sexual Offences Act 2003 2, 45
shouting 7, 17, 26
effect on children 17
teacher 17
significant harm 43
vs harm 43
Skinner, B.F. 33
Slee, P. 142
smacking 3
Smith, P.K. 30, 142
snogging 2
Snook, P.A. 4, 14, 24, 30, 140
social aggression 30
social networking 34
Social norms
abuse, and 21
socioeconomic level 36
spanking 3, 7, 17, 23
by parents 3
punishment, retaliation, or retribution 24
spare the rod; spoil the child 39
Special Educational Needs
see SEN
SSEA 36
state intervention 57
staying safe 52
Straus, M.A. 13, 14, 17, 22, 142
stress
teacher 35

## T

tawse 39
Taylor, C. 57, 142
teacher abuse

in Wikipedia 138
teacher as educator 31
teacher avoidance behaviour 17
teachers
respect for by pupils 31
teacher self-evaluation 7, 9, 69–75
teacher shouting 26
teacher stress 35
teaching
attainment, and 28
teenage pregnancies 2
and confidentiality 2
threats 18
thresholds 15
traditional teaching 32
tribal instinct 34
tribal urge 34
tribes
real 34
virtual 34

## U

ugly classroom experiences 92
UK liberalism 55
UK materialistic culture
parenting, and 56
UNCRC 8, 54, 58, 100–127, 130
application in schools 60–63
Children's Commissioner, and 58
domestic law, and 58
in school curriculum 59
use in legal proceedings 59
under-age pregnancies
sexual abuse, and 45
underage sexual activity 2
confidentiality, and 45
UNDRC 58, 96
plain language version 99
UN General Assembly 58, 59, 100, 130, 142
UNICEF 56–57, 142
United Nations Convention on the Rights of the Child
see UNCRC
United Nations Declaration on the Rights of the Child
see UNDRC
US Department of Justice 12, 143

## V

Vachss, A. 13, 143
verbal abuse
in Wikipedia 138
verbal belittling 36
verbal punishment 23
definition 26
Victoria Climbié 8, 51, 58
virtual tribes 34
Volpe, R. 30, 143

## W

Warin, J. 55, 56, 143
Wattenberg, W. 33
Webster's Dictionary 11, 12
well-being 43
child views on 56
UK bottom of the league 56
White, S. 51, 143
Wikipedia 10
articles 137–138
Wilson, K. 14, 41, 51, 143

## Z

zero tolerance 14

# Help with Training your People

It is a requirement for safeguarding training to include material about emotional abuse, and particularly, emotional abuse in the classroom.

There is very little material readily available to assist with that aspect of safeguarding training.

There are several contexts in which you may want training:

- at regular intervals, many schools have whole of school training attended by teachers and perhaps governors and other school workers - we have training materials available to supplement your normal safeguarding whole of school training;
- many local authorities provide courses for safeguarding - we have courses available to cover the emotional abuse aspects of safeguarding, which can be delivered as stand-alone courses, or to supplement existing courses;
- schools or school consortia may like to have a training session for teachers to use the self-assessment tools in this book - we can run sessions for such groups of teachers;
- a school, or school consortium, may wish to provide pupils with a self-assessment workshop - we can conduct a session to find out what your pupils really feel, and obtain input for management and planning;
- ClassroomEmotionalAbuse.com - the website associated with this book - can be used by individuals for self-assessment and to provide material for future editions of this book.

Whatever needs you have to become familiar with the ideas and self-assessment instruments in this book, you are welcome to contact us at info@classroomemotionalabuse.com to discuss what you would like to do, and how we can help you.